VAMPIRE
LEGENDS AND MYTHS

The Supernatural

VAMPIRE
LEGENDS AND MYTHS

Roxanne Hellman and Derek Hall

ROSEN
PUBLISHING®
New York

This edition first published in 2012 by:

The Rosen Publishing Group, Inc.
29 East 21st Street
New York, NY 10010

Additional end matter copyright ©
2012 by The Rosen Publishing Group,
Inc.

**Library of Congress
Cataloging-in-Publication Data**

Hellman, Roxanne.
Vampire legends and myths/Roxanne
Hellman, Derek Hall.
     p. cm.— (The supernatural)
Includes bibliographical references and
index.
ISBN 978-1-4488-5986-3 (lib. bdg.)
1. Vampires—United States. I. Hall,
Derek, 1930. II. Title.
BF1556.H45 2012
398'.45—dc23

                    2011030543

*Manufactured in the United States of
America*

CPSIA Compliance Information: Batch #W12YA: For
further information, contact Rosen Publishing, New York,
New York, at 1-800-237-9932.

Roxanne Hellman, Editor

CONTENTS

CHAPTER ONE

WHAT IS A VAMPIRE?

In the minds of most people, the very mention of the word "vampire" conjures up images of malignant entities in human form, coming in the dead of night and literally draining the life force from the bodies of unwitting, living victims by biting their throats in order to suck out their blood. And worse may follow, for the subjects of this horrible assault may themselves come under the vampires' thrall, making them succumb to the sickness that compels them to seek victims of their own.

Whether or not we believe in the existence of such creatures – and many insist that vampires truly move among us, and have done so since time immemorial – the phenomenon of taking the blood and tissues of another living animal is in reality commonplace, frequently encountered within the animal kingdom. When we are bitten by that annoying little mosquito, what she is

doing, in fact, is taking a small blood meal to aid the development of her young. Leeches are specially modified types of worms that feed solely on the

OPPOSITE: A victim may be so infected by a vampire as to become a vampire herself.

ABOVE: The common vampire bat (Desmodus rotundus) is the bloodsucker of the natural world.

RIGHT: A female vampire depicted in cartoon form.

LEFT: The vampire bat has a fierce set of teeth, which include the pointed incisors that allow it to penetrate its victim's skin.

BELOW LEFT: The lamprey is often parasitic, attaching itself to other fish in order to suck their blood.

BELOW: Leeches attach themselves to their hosts, remaining there until they become engorged with blood, at which point they fall off.

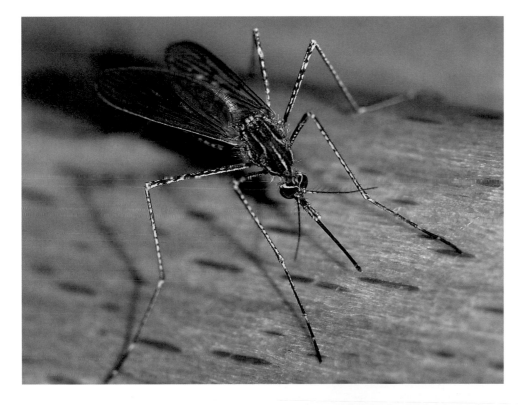

and legend) to penetrate the flesh of their victims.

There is one animal, however, that epitomizes the bloodsucker more than any other, and that is the vampire bat. *Desmodus rotundus* is widespread in tropical and subtropical regions of the Americas, and this small flying mammal is well-named, its mouth boasting a set of razor-sharp teeth used to get at its victim's blood before its long, thin, tubelike tongue laps it up. In the process of taking its meal, the vampire bat may transmit the deadly disease known as rabies, making it a creature to be doubly feared. Cattle are common targets of the bat's attentions, but human beings are

blood of other animals, while the eel-like hagfish and lampreys also find their food by latching onto, and then feeding from, the tissues of live prey, using their sharp, cutting teeth (so much the defining physical feature of the vampire of myth

ABOVE: The female mosquito takes blood from animals and humans to feed her young.

RIGHT: The eel-like hagfish is similar to the lamprey in its feeding habits.

not totally immune. Even the bat's lifestyle epitomizes the vampire's way of life, for it emerges from its dank, dark resting place only at night, flitting about in search of a likely victim. Then it goes about its work silently and efficiently, taking its fill of blood often without the victim being aware of the attack. It is perhaps no coincidence that the vampires of legend frequently seem to appear in the form of bats.

Vampires are considered by many to belong to the world of the undead. In other words, they are beings that are technically dead but still animate, a term that also describes other mythical or ephemeral beings. Ghosts are known as

LEFT: Ghosts fall into the category of incorporeal undead. This is supposedly the vaporous form of the Brown Lady, said to haunt Raynham Hall, in Norfolk, England.

OPPOSITE LEFT: Zombies, or reanimated dead, from the 1968 movie, The Night of the Living Dead.

OPPOSITE RIGHT: A first-edition cover of Bram Stoker's famous novel, Dracula.

Stoker's seminal 1897 novel, *Dracula,* the vampiric creature is sometimes to be seen in the form of a huge wolflike creature, but at other times appears in the room of his "guest" in a human, physical form, while casting no reflection in a mirror. Little wonder, then, that vampires make such fearsome and elusive adversaries, not only for those who fall victim to their evil ways, but also for those seeking to eradicate them from the world.

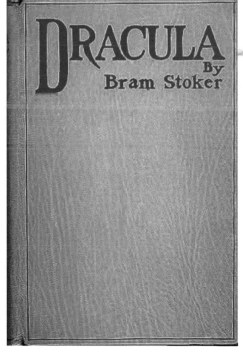

incorporeal entities; in other words, they have no substance or body although they can manifest themselves in vaporous forms that may be visible to human beings. Because they lack substance, ghosts cannot physically touch or move objects, but their lack of a material existence allows them to pass without hindrance through solid objects such as brick walls.

Vampires, on the other hand, along with other well-documented forms of undead creatures, such as zombies, are referred to as corporeal entities; in other words, they appear to have physical bodies. Despite this physicality, however, it is not unknown for vampires sometimes to assume a mantle of invisibility or to take the form of other creatures, such as wolves. In Bram

VAMPIRE LEGENDS AND MYTHS

Vampire Characteristics

According to some, vampires have special powers that enable them to do their sinister work. They are extremely strong, utilizing this strength either to help them subdue unwilling victims or to ward off their adversaries. Their senses of hearing and smell are also highly developed, enabling them to pinpoint their victims at a distance. Vampires are

BELOW: Vampires are able to target their victims from a distance.

OPPOSITE: Vampires are said to be able to control cats, rats, and snakes.

also able to move at great speed, and some can fly, and they have ways to conceal their actual presence. They move silently, which again allows them to go about their activities virtually undetected.

Vampires need blood to maintain their existence, and may also take the blood of animals in the absence of human victims. Vampires may sometimes seek eye contact, inducing a temporary hypnotic state in their victims before attacking them, which is why looking directly into a vampire's eyes must strictly be avoided. It is said that some vampires are capable even of mass

hypnosis, and that the ability to mind-read is not beyond their capabilities. Allusion has already been made to the fact that the attentions of a vampire can make the victim a vampire in turn, but the effect can go much farther than this, turning the victim into the vampire's abject slave.

Thus vampires may force their human servants to help them in their nefarious deeds. Such people usually fall under the vampire's spell in ritualized stages, beginning with eye contact and ending in mutual blood-drinking. Vampires may also summon up other creatures to do their bidding, such as snakes, cats, and rats. It is also said that the power of the vampire increases after several centuries of existence, and that some may attain "master" status when, by now possessing the full range of special abilities, they are able to exert control over other, lesser vampires. Thus there exists a hierarchy of sorts within "vampire society," where lesser vampires

LEFT & OPPOSITE: A vampire may hypnotize its victim before going for the throat.

must defer to those of higher rank, and may need to seek permission, for example, before entering territory already in the control of their masters.

Vampires shun the light, and must operate only under the cover of darkness. A few vampires, however, while active during the day, must confine themselves to the shadows, avoiding exposure to full sunlight. Most vampires prefer to seek the sanctuary of a tomb or similar place, until they are ready to rise up and begin their quest. Despite the powers that vampires are said to possess, there are, as we shall later discover, ways of dealing with them and thwarting their evil intent.

But once the fantasy, and even the romanticism that seem to have attached themselves to the cult are stripped away, we are left simply with the definition of a vampire as a preternatural (in other words, abnormal or supernatural) being

Vampires usually operate under the cover of darkness, which is the time when the nightmarish fears, worst imaginings, and most lurid suspicions of their victims are at their most pronounced.

LEFT: Dark, dank crypts make the perfect vampire lair during the daylight hours.

BELOW & OPPOSITE: Vampires traditionally spend their days in the coffins in which they were buried.

believed to be living people. If our description of a vampire as a bloodsucking entity is to be our guide, furthermore, then many different, strange and ghastly creatures will emerge during the course of our journey through these pages; in the multitude of cultures that tell of such nightmarish

in the form of a reanimated corpse, ruthlessly intent on keeping itself alive. To further enhance an already notorious reputation, vampires seem disposed to rest by day in dark and fetid places, rising from their lairs only under the cover of night, which is the time when our nightmarish fears, worst imaginings, and most lurid suspicions are at their height. But even the suggestion that vampires are the dead brought back to life is not as clear-cut as it might seem, for in certain cultures vampires are

fiends, it will soon be apparent that the activities of vampires, in their many forms, seem to know no bounds where pure evil is concerned.

Despite the ancient origins of the belief in such unlikely creatures, time has done nothing to diminish our morbid interest in, and indeed fear of, these beings of our most dread imaginings. Today, the word "vampire" still persists in everyday language; indeed, it has been transferred to real objects, from mighty bomber aircraft and small nocturnal bats to describing a particular sort of predatory woman. Today we continue to feed this awful fascination with ever more books, films, and television series; these are designed to chill and thrill us in equal measure, to a point when our strange preoccupation with vampires seems never likely to be satisfied.

The Changing Form of Vampires

Vampires have appeared in many guises throughout history. In early folklore, they were often depicted as bloated, shroud-clad figures with dark or ruddy complexions, this, no doubt, being the result of disinterring corpses suspected

of being vampires, which will be examined later. From the beginning of the 19th century, however, vampires seem to have changed their appearance, in that they are now depicted as pale, gaunt creatures, looking as though their dreadful lifestyle has drained and exhausted them, giving them the same unearthly pallor as their abused victims.

The irresistible force that drives the vampire to sate its perpetual hunger is no more apparent than in the 1922 silent movie, *Nosferatu*, in which the vampire is depicted as a pale, thin, goblin-eared, long-taloned entity of extremely repellent mien and with equally unsavory habits. This classic idea was taken a step farther in *Salem's Lot,* the first television adaptation, in 1979, of Stephen King's dark and disturbing tale of vampires in modern-day America. Here, the Master, the principal vampire figure, is clearly based on the one seen more than 50 years earlier in *Nosferatu*, but made into an even more malevolent embodiment of depravity

Images of Nosferatu from the 1922 silent movie of the same name. The film was essentially an unauthorized adaptation of Bram Stoker's Dracula, with names and other details changed.

WHAT IS A VAMPIRE?

and evil. Here is a huge and powerful being that is physically abhorrent, scarcely human in form, and given to uttering inhuman sounds.

The mythology of some cultures, existing in parts of South-East Asia such as Malaysia, is littered with all manner of hideous vampirelike entities, some of which can detach their heads from their bodies at will and send them flying off into the night to satisfy the creatures' lust for blood.

More recent vampires, such as those that appear in *Buffy the Vampire Slayer*,

and in other such films and television series, and benefiting not only from the advanced skills of modern makeup artists but also from computer-generated imagery, have appeared in a myriad of imaginative and repulsive guises. And who is to say which of the aforementioned is the more accurate? If vampires are able to change their shapes, taking the forms of animals such as bats, then there is no reason why they cannot be anything they choose. Or perhaps, like the creatures in the world with which

LEFT: The Filipina mananangal resembles the Malasian penanggalan, described as an older, beautiful woman. It is capable of severing its upper torso from the rest of its body in order to fly into the night on huge batlike wings to prey on unsuspecting pregnant women. It uses its long tongue, rather like a proboscis, to suck at the hearts of fetuses or the blood of its sleeping victims.

BELOW: A still from Buffy the Vampire Slayer.

Courtesy of Mutant Enemy/Capital Pictures

23

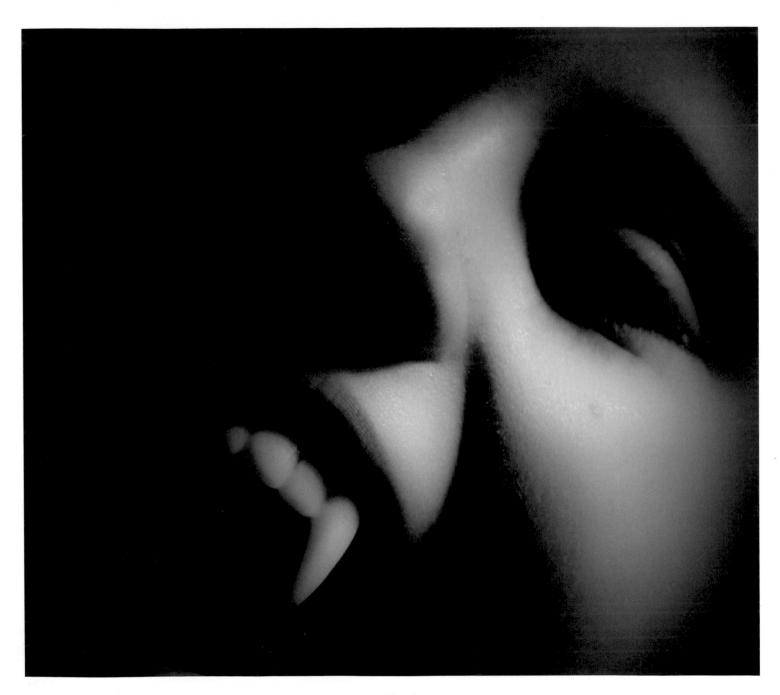

WHAT IS A VAMPIRE?

OPPOSITE: *Portrait of a vampire, its teeth bared and ready for action.*

LEFT: *The red eye of a vampire.*

BELOW: *Christopher Lee, the British actor, was a particularly effective Count Dracula.*

genre in general. In these portrayals Dracula, when not in full bloodsucking mode, appears as a tall, suave, slightly sinister character, resplendent in his dark evening clothes and cloak, as if ready for a night out at the opera.

we are familiar, it may be that there are simply many different species of vampire.

According to some superstitions, especially those emanating from places such as south-eastern Europe, inanimate objects, such as farm tools or even fruit, are able to become vampires under the appropriate conditions – for example, when left outside on the eve of a full moon. Far-fetched though this may seem, is this really any more fantastic than the idea of the living dead, destined to be the plague of mankind into eternity?

Many depictions of the vampire will be examined in later chapters, ranging from dark and disturbing Gothic renderings to lighthearted comical and cartoon offerings. But it would be impossible to continue without reference to what are arguably two of the most famous of all such portrayals, for each in their own way contributes to the particular style evident in that most famous of vampires, Count Dracula, becoming not only his exemplars for years to come, but also for the vampire

In 1931 the Hungarian actor Bela Lugosi starred as Dracula in the film version of a 1927 Broadway production, based on Bram Stoker's novel. With his distinctive looks and pronounced accent, together with an authentic Transylvanian heritage, Lugosi's was probably the definitive version, despite being a younger version of the white-haired and mustachioed character of the original novel. The second to make the role his own was the British actor Christopher Lee who starred in the legendary Hammer Horror productions of the 1950s, 1960s, and 1970s. Here again, Dracula is a tall, urbane character with the same dark, slicked-back hair and seemingly impeccable manners, even though there is the distinct feeling he could do with getting out in the fresh air a little more often. But in full vampire mode, the famous count again displays the bloodlust typical of the genre when,

OPPOSITE: Vampires are credited with shape-shifting powers, able to turn themselves into bats or other animals at will.

RIGHT: Count Dracula in more jocular mode.

BELOW: Varney the Vampire or The Feast of Blood was a mid-Victorian Gothic horror story by James Malcolm Rymer, which first appeared in 1845-47 in a series of pamphlets generally referred to as penny dreadfuls, on account of their cheapness and typically gruesome contents. It was published in book form in 1847, the original edition being of epic proportions, and was a major influence on later vampire fiction, particularly Bram Stoker's Dracula of 1897.

his pointed incisors bared for action, he prepares to attack his victim.

It is interesting to note, however, how the portrayal of the vampire in popular culture has changed and continues to change. And as it changes, so the predator-prey dynamic changes with it. Many of the vampire tales, that captured the attention of 18th-century western Europeans, involved peasant communities living in places such as south-eastern Europe. Such communities, it seemed, were often troubled by one or more of their own kind returning from the dead to prey on their relatives, with deceased husbands attacking living members of their own families, and so on. Later, 18th- and 19th-century writers had vampires coming from more noble stock, with Count Dracula, for example, being the focus of the local peasantry's awe and fear. There are many other high-born vampires, such as Sir Francis Varney, Lord Ruthven, and Lord Otto Goetzi, in which instances the voracious vampires see the "lower orders" as their rightful prey, not unlike the *droit du seigneur*, or the right of a feudal lord to have sexual intercourse with a vassal's bride on her wedding night. In recent times, the curse of the vampire appears to have gone full circle, with those so infected – typically, average teenagers, adolescents, or young adults – frequently seeing their peers as potential victims.

The Psychology of Vampirism

How is it that the vampire – or at least the concept of vampirism, for the word itself only came into common usage less than 300 years ago – has been able to insinuate itself so firmly, and for so long, into the psyche of mankind? We fear this seductive embodiment of lust and evil that forces us to yield the very lifeblood from our bodies, yet

Count Dracula and other vampires are often depicted as debonair gentlemen on the surface, but with a blood-thirsty alter ego.

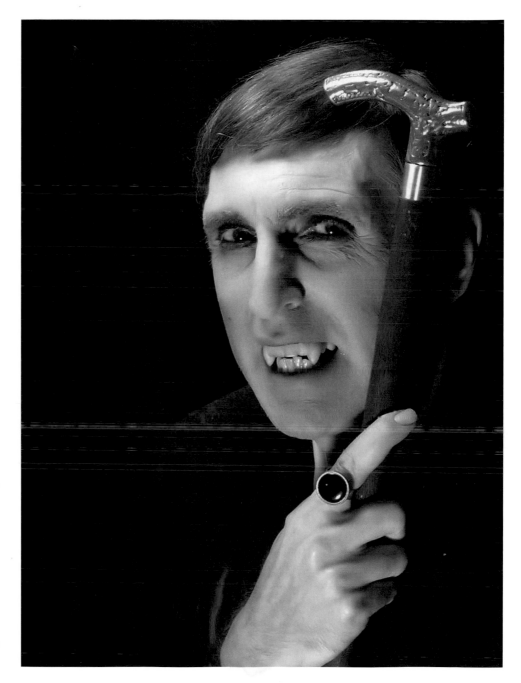

throughout history countless cultures
seem to have recognized the
inherent in the concept by
blood sacrifices to the gods
of appeasing them and perpetuating

f. Some modern psychologists have
mpted to shed light on the subject by
ng the proposition that people
fy with immortal vampires because
ng so they conquer or, at the very

least, temporarily escape from, their own
fears of dying.

The Welsh psychoanalyst Ernest
Jones, who among other achievements
became president of the International

Psychoanalytic Association and was the official biographer of the great Sigmund Freud, wrote in his 1931 book, *On the Nightmare*, that vampires seem to symbolize some of our subconscious drives and defense mechanisms. He argued that emotions, such as guilt, love and hate, can stimulate thoughts concerning the return of the dead from the grave, because in the same way that mourners yearn for the return of the dead, so the dead have a craving to return. This may be the underlying reason for the belief that vampires first visit their spouses and other family members; what is more likely, of course, is that a particular virulent and contagious disease (the real cause of the deaths involved in many vampire myths) would have passed through the family from one to another, making them succumb, in turn, as they saw it, to the "overtures" of a vampire.

The image of the vampire swings between that of the grotesque, alarming and lustful monster, intent on satisfying its bloodlust, to one in which the relationship between vampire and victim suggests strong sexual attraction.

WHAT IS A VAMPIRE?

OPPOSITE: Female vampires are as predatory as their male counterparts.

RIGHT: Lilith, by James Wells Champney, a female demon of Hebrew folklore who preyed on newborn children. She is thought to be Adam's first wife until dispossessed by Eve.

Freud himself took this a stage farther, with the proposal that where a subconscious guilt existed concerning a relationship, the desire for a reunion might be corrupted by anxiety. This, in turn, could lead to feelings of repression and morbid dread. From this, Jones extrapolated that the initial wish for a sexual reunion might be subverted by feelings of fear, which would lead to love being replaced by sadistic feelings, the loved one being replaced by an unknown entity.

Vampires can also be seen to represent the dark side of the human condition. Vampiric female demons, such as Lilith, are regarded as the antithesis of good wives and mothers, in that they are intent on seducing men other than their husbands and devouring babies or young children – sometimes while they are still in the womb. Thus, by

using preternatural figures to define evil, people are able to externalize their own wicked tendencies. It is also human nature to sublimate our fears by casting the threat, these fears seem to pose, in the form of monsters, a trait that has existed throughout history.

It seems, however, that the vampire lifestyle is not confined to the undead alone. History is littered with examples of real-life murderers who have seemingly been consumed by bloodlust. A few of these are described below, but who knows how many more have been encouraged to kill by a desire for their victims' blood? One of the most notorious of these was Countess Elizabeth Báthory, who died in 1614, and became known for her crimes as the "Blood Countess," the "Bloody Lady of Cachtice," and even "Countess Dracula." Most of her crimes were committed in what was then the kingdom of Hungary, but which is now Slovakia. She was accused of torturing and killing literally hundreds of girls and women – perhaps as many as 650 or more – although the number for which she was convicted at her trial was "only" 80! The case has

given rise probably to fictional accounts of how the countess bathed in the blood of virgins in order to retain her youth, and has also drawn comparisons with the bloody deeds of the notorious Vlad Tepes of Wallachia (Chapter 8), who was himself thought by many to be the inspiration for the fictional Count

Dracula. It was feared at the time that the trial and possible execution of such a high-ranking person as the countess might reflect badly on the nobility, so Elizabeth Báthory was imprisoned in her castle while the courts deliberated her fate. But four years into her incarceration she was found dead.

On July 2, 1931, the German serial killer Peter Kürten was executed by guillotine in Cologne. His case had been widely reported in the press at the time, which referred to him as the "Vampire of Düsseldorf," where many of his crimes took place. He was found guilty of many assaults as well as for the murder of at least nine people and the attempted murder of seven more over a

period of at least 17 years, and possibly more. He was eventually arrested in 1930, and confessed at his trial to no fewer than 79 offenses. It appears that what motivated him to murder was to see his victims' blood, the sight of which aroused him sexually.

Then, in 1932, a 32 year old prostitute was found murdered in her tiny flat in the Atlas area of Stockholm, Sweden. The police confirmed she had been dead for several days, that her skull had been crushed, and that someone had been drinking her blood. This "Vampire

OPPOSITE: Cachtice Castle, where Elizabeth Báthory is reputed to have tortured and murdered hundreds of women and children.

ABOVE RIGHT: Elizabeth Báthory is said to have bathed in the blood of her victims in order to preserve her youthful beauty.

RIGHT: Peter Kürten, the "Vampire of Düsseldorf."

Murder Case" was never solved, but the perpetrator of the crime was dubbed the "Atlas Vampire."

More recently, the case of the American serial killer Richard Chase once again brought real-life vampirism to the attention of the general public. Here was a person so depraved and sadistic that he became known as the "Vampire of Sacramento." A chronic drug-user, with a history of family abuse and dysfunctional behavior, Chase also developed acute hypochondria as well as other even more unusual and irrational behavioral symptoms, including extreme paranoia. He began killing and disembowelling animals in order to eat

them raw, sometimes blending the body parts with soft drinks. In 1975 he was committed to a mental institution where he became ill after injecting rabbit's blood into his veins. Staff at the institution dubbed him "Dracula" when it was discovered that he had been drinking the blood of captured birds.

Then, in December 1977, following his release, he embarked on a month-long killing spree that continued until January 1978. During this orgy of death, in which Chase killed six people, including a 22-month-old child, he bathed in the blood of one of his victims and drank the blood of several others; he also feasted on various body parts, including a brain. He was arrested, was brought to trial, and was deemed sufficiently sane to have committed the murders in a premeditated fashion that would warrant the death penalty. In December 1980, however, a prison guard discovered Chase lying dead on his bed. A subsequent autopsy determined he had died from a self-inflicted drug overdose; it seems he had been storing up antidepressants that had been prescribed to him for several weeks.

The notion of the handsome, sexy vampire, as represented opposite, is a far cry from the reality of such psychotic serial killers as Richard Chase (pictured below left), who murdered then cannibalized some of his many victims.

While we can conjecture the meaning and mythology of vampirism, when true examples of such behavior come to light, which may also involve cannibalism, the subject becomes too distressing to contemplate. It is convenient to think that most such real-life cases are the result of deviancy caused by insanity, but it has also been the cultural norm in many societies, in Papua New Guinea, for example, to feast on the flesh and blood of others. In recent times there have also been disturbing reports of soldiers in African countries, such as the Democratic Republic of Congo and Liberia, eating human body parts in order to intimidate others, and of despotic leaders consuming the flesh of their victims. One of the cultural reasons often cited, perhaps in the case of an enemy warrior captured in battle, is that to cannibalize him will bring extra vigor and longevity

to the perpetrator (an argument not that much different from the one used to explain vampirism).

Cannibalism may also occur as a sign of the total supremacy of the victor over the defeated. And, of course, it may also be because the victim is a ready source of nourishment in the absence of normal food – one of the reasons why in some cultures, where cannibalism has long been practiced, human flesh is referred to as "long pig." Extreme hunger, prompting the desperate need to resort to human flesh for the purpose of survival has occurred countless times throughout history, as well as in the recent past, when, in a well-documented case, a group of people on a Uruguayan Air Force flight were stranded after their aircraft crashed in the remote Andes Mountains in 1972.

Seduction and the Vampire

The image of the vampire swings between that of the grotesque, alarming, and lustful monster, intent on doing nothing more than using its victim to satisfy its bloodlust, to one in which the relationship between vampire and victim

suggests a strong attraction. *The Vampire* (page 40), for example, the best-known work of the British painter Sir Philip Burne-Jones, who died in 1926, depicts a beautiful, scantily-clad young woman with an unconscious man. It is thought that the woman in the painting was based on the actress Mrs. Patrick Campbell, with whom Burne-Jones is

said to have been romantically involved. To make the case more strongly: the

ABOVE: Cannibalism was once the cultural norm in Papua New Guinea and elsewhere.

OPPOSITE: More often than not, modern-day vampires are depicted as alluring and sexually attractive.

word "vamp," an abbreviated form of vampire, is commonly used to describe a woman who uses her feminine charms to seduce and exploit men. In recent years, moreover, all manner of imaginative books and exquisitely produced films and television series have appeared, aimed especially at the teen romance market, whose storylines are based primarily on the strong sexual chemistry that exists between young, attractive mortals and the even more impossibly attractive vampires that they encounter (*see* Chapter Eleven).

In 1819, the Italian-English author John William Polidori wrote a short story entitled "The Vampyre," which unfortunately was passed off as the work of Lord Byron when it was published in *New Monthly Magazine*. In it, a young man, by the name of Aubrey, unwittingly encounters one of the undead, and a trail of death is the result. This sinister entity, going by the name of Lord Ruthven, is to all intents and purposes a normal man, albeit with a mysterious past, and a member of London's high society. Later, when Aubrey is in Greece, he becomes attracted to Ianthe, an

innkeeper's daughter, who recounts to him a vampire legend, and soon afterwards Ruthven murders her. Not knowing that it is a vampire that has killed his beloved, Aubrey agrees to join Ruthven on his travels. On their journey,

LEFT: The Vampire, by Sir Philip Burne-Jones.

ABOVE: Philip Burne-Jones (1861-1926).

however, bandits set upon them and Ruthven is mortally wounded. Before dying, Ruthven asks Aubrey to swear an oath he will not divulge anything about him for a year and a day – not even the news of his death.

Aubrey returns to London and is astonished when, some time later, he again encounters Ruthven, looking very much alive and well. But he is reminded of the oath he swore, and therefore says nothing. Ruthven then seduces Aubrey's sister, which poor Aubrey is unable to prevent, causing him to suffer a mental breakdown as a result. A date is set for the wedding of Ruthven and Aubrey's sister; it is the day that the oath of silence comes to an end. Meanwhile, Aubrey conveys what he knows about Ruthven in a letter to his sister before dying himself. Unfortunately, the letter fails to arrive in time and the wedding goes ahead as planned. Ruthven kills his new wife on their wedding night and escapes.

John William Polidori – the author of a short story entitled "The Vampyre" – painted by F.G. Gainsford, c.1816.

WHAT IS A VAMPIRE?

OPPOSITE, LEFT, & PAGES 44 & 45: Images of vamps. The word "vamp" is an abbreviation of "vampire," used to describe a predatory woman who uses sexual attraction to exploit men.

"The Vampyre" was probably the inspiration for the so-called romantic vampire genre that followed, as well as being the first to combine the vampire tradition with this form of literature. And to return to the Dracula of Hammer Horror films, of course, no one could mistake the sexual overtones present in the relationship between the tall, seductive count and his beautiful, buxom victims!

Herein lies a great paradox: on the one hand there is the morbid fear of a night creature draining us of our lifeblood, and on the other, the willing submission to a lustful lover with exactly the same intention in mind. Could it be possible that the underlying eroticism of some aspects of vampirism may be due to the fact that here is an expression of a union so strong and so binding that the lovers desire more than mere intercourse, being desirous instead of

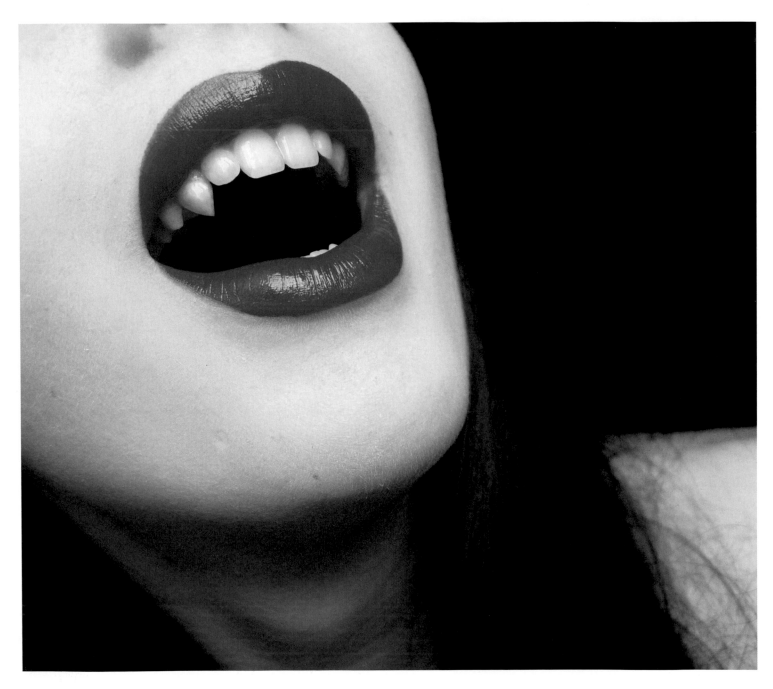

sharing the life force that runs through the veins of both. Is a harmless love bite, in reality, symbolic of our covert desire to be vampires? Is our aversion to vampires merely our suppressed fear of having our hearts and souls stolen by another? And is the transformation into a vampire oneself merely a sign that the sublime conjunction is now complete, and that vampire and victim have in some way become one another?

Might it not also be that the more hideous manifestations of vampirism, promulgated throughout history and folklore, have more to do with religious or moral influences intended to moderate our sexual excesses and make us live in fear of what the afterlife may hold? And might it also be intended to prevent us from giving up our blood to another, in case we encourage or provide them with the means of gaining immortality?

CHAPTER TWO
THE ORIGINS OF VAMPIRES

Some say vampires are as old as the world itself, and legends of vampires are indeed to be found throughout recorded history. Ancient civilizations, such as those of the Babylonians, Egyptians, Greeks, and Romans, all refer to blood-drinking spirits and other entities, as do more recent cultures from as far apart as Asia and Europe. In the West, Romania appears to be an important point of origin and a major stronghold.

Despite the fact that creatures with vampirelike tendencies had been documented from very early times in many parts of the world, the actual term "vampire" did not come into common usage until the 1730s, when alleged vampiric activities in south-eastern Europe were brought to the

Vampires were believed to be the reanimated corpses of evil-doers, suicides, or witches.

LEFT: According to both Slavic and Chinese folklore, a deceased person will become one of the undead if an animal, such as a dog, jumps over the corpse.

OPPOSITE & PAGE 50: Modern vampire mythology appears to have originated and be most persistent in eastern Europe, where ancient castles, jagged mountains, and deep forests are imagined to harbor dark secrets.

wider attention of people in other parts of the continent. Vampires were widely considered to be the reanimated corpses of evil-doers, suicides, or sorcerers and witches. It was also believed that vampirelike creatures could come into being through a malevolent spirit inhabiting and possessing a corpse, or through someone having been bitten by a vampire themselves. In places, the belief in these incidences was so great that mass panic broke out, and people suspected of vampirism were publicly executed in an attempt to put a stop to their activities.

Given the long historical documentation and wide-ranging incidences of vampires in world folklore, it is not surprising to find that the

circumstances giving rise to vampiric generation are equally ancient and diverse. In both Slavic and Chinese folklore it is said that any corpse that is jumped over by an animal, such as a cat or a dog, is destined to become one of the undead. Bodies with wounds untreated with boiling water were also at risk of suffering the same dark fate. Russian folklore has it that vampires were once people who had been witches or who had argued with the Church

when alive. What many of these beliefs have in common is that a vampire can materialize as the result of a body being improperly buried or by some unfortunate oversight in the after-death ritual. In any case, religion and vampirism seem to be closely linked.

ABOVE: In Slavic folklore, a domovoi is a house spirit. Domovye are masculine, typically small, and sometimes covered in hair. They often have tails or little horns.

Transylvania and the Carpathian Mountains seem to have inspired a particularly strong folkloric tradition.

The Slavic Influence

When considering the origins of the "modern" vampire tradition, we find ourselves returning, time and again, to the Slavic strongholds of south-eastern and eastern Europe in our search for enlightenment. But why should this be so? Despite the fact that many cultures have vampiric superstitions, it is the Slavic form of the phenomenon, more than any other, that seems to have insinuated itself into our culture and psyche. The reasons can probably be traced back to the ways in which pre-Christianized Slavic people viewed the spiritual world, as well as their concept of the afterlife. Even after the advent of Christianity to the region, many of the old pagan rituals and beliefs were still followed. These included the worship of ancestors, the belief that spirit forms were at large in the house, and certain notions concerning the fate of the soul after death.

Spirits and demons once played an important role in Slav culture, pervading the lives of the people and influencing many aspects of their everyday existence. Not all spirits were evil, however; some could be helpful, while others were malevolent and harmful. The fact that these spirits were deemed to be so influential in the lives of ordinary people meant that they felt obliged to please and appease the spirits in order to prevent them from causing mischief or worse.

There were several different types of these entities, some of which are described here. First there is the house spirit, the *domovoi* – a small, often horned, masculine, hairy creature, said to inhabit every house, its favorite resting-places being thresholds beneath doors or under kitchen stoves. Some *domovye* are said to assume the appearance of current or previous owners of the house. Usually benign and considered to be the guardians of the dwelling, folklore has it

A kikimora, thought to be the spirit of an unbaptized child or aborted fetus, is by tradition married to a domovoi.

that there is a darker side to the *domovoi,* in that it will often torment animals it does not like and may play unpleasant tricks on the family. But most people prefer to live in harmony with their *domovoi,* especially as it is thought to have oracular powers.

Another house spirit, the female *kikimora,* is by tradition said to be married to a *domovoi,* and is thought to be the spirit of an unbaptized child or an aborted fetus. According to one macabre legend, when a woman dies, all her aborted fetuses visit her and take her soul to hell. In some artistic

ABOVE: Rusalki are mermaidlike demons that live in the water.

ABOVE RIGHT: Antonín Dvořák (1841–1904).

RIGHT: Růžena Maturová, the first Rusalka in Dvořák's opera of the same name.

interpretations, the *kikimora* is depicted as an individual with a long, pointed snout, her long ears peeping out from beneath a peasant's shawl. She also has long, clawed fingers and feet resembling those of a chicken. The *kikimora* is said to busy herself looking after chickens and doing housework. To see her spinning is an omen that the death will soon follow of the person witnessing this event.

A *rusalka* is a female ghost, mermaidlike demon, or succubus that inhabits water. Most traditions describe her as a beautiful fish-woman living on the riverbed. At dead of night, she leaves the water to climb bankside trees or dance in the meadows, mesmerizing any handsome men she encounters with her singing and dancing, before leading them away to live with her. The *rusalka* is usually described as having green or golden hair, which some legends say is always wet, for she would die if it were ever to dry out. She always carries her comb with her, and uses it to conjure up water whenever she needs it. *Rusalki* are thought to be at their most dangerous during the Rusalka Week festival held in early June.

OPPOSITE: *The vodianoi is a male water spirit with a fish tail and webbed paws.*

ABOVE: *Nymphs Finding the Head of Orpheus, by John William Waterhouse (1900). Vilas are Slavic nymphs with diverse habitats that include water.*

The *vodianoi* is a male water spirit. Legend has it that he is an old, naked man with a green beard and long hair, his body coated with algae, mud, and fish scales. Instead of hands, he has webbed paws, and he has a fish's tail instead of legs. Like the *rusalka*, the *vodianoi* was often implicated in local drownings. When angered, he is reputed to break dams and damage watermills.

Another spirit being, the *vila*, is the Slavic version of a nymph with power over storms, which she likes to bring down on travellers. She lives in places as diverse as fields, oceans, trees, and clouds, and can appear in a variety of

forms, as a swan, a horse, a wolf, a snake or even a beautiful woman. *Vilas* are thought to be the spirits of women who have led frivolous lives and have been left to drift somewhere between the real world and the afterlife. Not only are they fierce warriors, making the ground shake when engaged in battle, but they also have powers to see into the future and to heal the sick. The fairy rings sometimes seen in grass are supposed to be the places where they have danced; these should not be stepped upon, otherwise bad luck will be bound to ensue.

The Slavs believed in a clear distinction between the body and the soul. While the body might perish after death, the soul was deemed to be

LEFT: Vilas can shape-shift into many forms such as swans or other animals.

OPPOSITE ABOVE: It is said that fairy rings appear where vilas have danced.

OPPOSITE BELOW: In Slavic tradition, a deceased person's door or window was left open for 40 days, allowing their soul to wander to and fro at will.

children left unbaptized or people convicted of a heinous crime. What could also apply if the burial ritual was not carried out properly was that the body could become the possession of other unclean souls or spirits. It was from these deep-seated fears and beliefs that the Slavic tradition of the *vampir* arose, this being an unclean spirit in possession of a dead body. The undead entity is jealous and vengeful towards the living, being in need of their blood in order to perpetuate its own existence.

indestructible. The belief was that the soul left the body, following death, to roam the neighborhood for 40 days before it moved on to its eternal resting-place. For this reason, doors or windows in the house or workplace of the deceased would be left open so that the soul could wander to and fro at will. At this time, it was also thought that the soul could re-enter the body of the deceased. Because the wandering soul could have either a benign or a malevolent influence at this critical period, much care was taken to ensure that burial rites were carried out correctly, thus protecting the soul's peace and purity as it passed from the body. In some cases a soul might be rendered "unclean" after death, and this applied to those who had met violent deaths, or to

LEFT: A woodcut depicting the Great Plague of London. Contagion may often have been confused with vampiric activity.

OPPOSITE: Bodies were exhumed from graves as people searched for proof of vampire activity.

The Body After Death

Scientific knowledge is forever moving forward. Who could have imagined, when the first faltering flight of a powered aircraft took place in 1903, that by 1969 human beings would walk on the Moon? Until well into the 20th century, little was known of antibiotics, and many surgical procedures that are considered routine today were still beyond the scope, or even the imagination, of physicians. As recently as the 1850s, there was no true understanding of the real causes of the devastating outbreaks of deadly typhoid that afflicted the great city of London. Imagine, then, how little was known about the human body by a peasant people hundreds of years ago, and particularly of the physiological and biological events that occur within the body following death.

Among communities where vampirism was thought to exist, the common practice was to dig up the body of the suspected person in order to examine it. If the body showed what were considered to be signs of vampirism, then it would be subjected to a series of procedures intended to render it incapable of continuing with its dire and fearful activities. Unfortunately, because of the lack of scientific knowledge of such matters at the time, many of the "signs" that were taken to

be irrefutable proof were no more than the completely normal processes that ensue when a body is laid to rest in the ground. For example, the corpse begins to swell as bacteria start to decompose the body and produce gases. This can lead not only to a body seeming plumper than it was at the point of death, but can also convey to the uninitiated that they are looking at a being so sated with its victim's blood that it has even gained in weight! In some cases, the exhumed body may seem not to have decomposed at all; in fact, one of the "victims" of Arnold Paole (*see* page 95 et seq.) looked even healthier than she had been when alive. This may be because the skin begins to turn reddish or purplish during decomposition, producing the so-called "healthy" countenance rather than the expected deathly pallor. This would go a long way towards explaining the early descriptions of vampires as being bloated and red of face.

The pressure of the gases generated in the body can also force blood from the body orifices, so that it collects around the eyes, nose and mouth. Here we probably see the "evidence" of a vampire's ghastly activities; in other words, what further proof was needed when the beast still had its victim's blood in its mouth? Another feature associated with the disinterred corpse, and yet another supposed sign that life may be continuing after death, especially in the eyes of the superstitious, is the fact that the teeth, nails, and even the hair still appear to be growing. This, however, is an illusion caused when body tissues lose fluids and contract, thereby exposing the roots of the structures in question and making them appear longer. At a certain point in the process of decomposition, the nails fall off and the skin begins to peel away. This exposes both the nail beds and the dermis of the skin (the tissue beneath the outer skin layer), both of which natural processes can be taken to be signs of old tissue being shed and new growth taking place.

Finally, when all or most of these frightening observations had been duly

Modern notions of what vampires look like tend to parallel the popular images of actors in films and television rather than those of traditional folklore.

noted, it fell on those responsible for the task to ensure that, next time around, the body would be buried having been freed from its vampiric controller. One of the most widely used procedures was to drive a stake through the heart of the corpse. But even this act often helped to reinforce the widely accepted view that a vampire was in their midst, for the action of driving the stake into the body could elicit groans or similar sounds as the body gases were forced over the vocal cords, and residual blood in the heart, veins, or arteries was made to seep from the body in what were regarded as further signs of something not quite dead.

In time, of course, the processes of decomposition – aided no doubt by the activities of myriad soil-dwelling creatures – would reach a point of putrefaction, breakdown, and decay whereby no one could judge the corpse to have been

RIGHT: In some cases, scythes were placed near to a grave ...

OPPOSITE: ... while in others, a stake would be driven through the heart to prevent the corpse from rising again.

morbidly enjoying some sort of nourishing afterlife. Enough exhumations seem to have been carried out fast enough, however, for this stage not to have been reached, and thus for the onlookers to conclude that here indeed was an active vampire.

Defeating Vampires

It would seem that a common belief, built on fear, underlies all the unlikely explanations for the existence of vampires. Not only do we fear the act of dying, but we also fear the possibility that the corpse, committed to rest in the ground, will not remain there unless particular rituals, designed to ensure that this does not happen, are followed. Many of these fears simply have their origins in the ignorance once prevalent concerning the process of decay that ensues once the body is buried. At one

time, burying a corpse upside-down was widely seen as a way of making sure it would never get out of the grave again, while objects, such as scythes and sickles, were sometimes placed near to the grave to appease any demons about to enter the body and to prevent it from rising again. In Ancient Greece, a coin would be placed in the corpse's mouth before burial. Some believe this was intended as payment for the ferryman, Charon, who was responsible for transporting the body across the River Styx, the boundary between Earth and the Underworld, to Hades. Others, however, have argued that the coin was for warding off evil spirits that might otherwise enter the body – a clear reference to the fear that

vampirism might otherwise ensue. The placing of coins or other items in the coffin with the corpse is a widespread

LEFT: Prehistoric burial mounds were covered with heavy stones to prevent vampires from escaping.

ABOVE: In some cultures, poppy seeds, sand, or millet are used to distract vampires.

OPPOSITE & OVERLEAF: In the hands of the true believer, crucifixes, rosary beads, and other religious artifacts have the power to stop vampires in their tracks.

Just as the vampire drinks the sinner's blood and possesses and devours his spirit, so the righteous Christian partakes of Christ's transubstantiated body and blood in the Eucharist (left) to be filled with His holiness.

In modern Greek folklore there are examples of steps being taken to combat *vrykolakas*, these being malevolent, undead creatures generally equated with the vampires of neighboring Slavic countries. To avoid the possibility of a

practice in many cultures, and is seen in many parts of the world to this day.

In some places, there appears to be a strong moral link between a person's behavior when alive and their likelihood of returning as a vampire after death. In parts of eastern Europe, for example, those who had been alcoholics were sometimes dug up again following their burial. They would then have a stake driven through their body, their head would be cut off, and their hearts removed. These actions, it was hoped, would divert the deceased from following the path of vampirism because the devil would be prevented from reanimating the corpse. The chances of becoming a vampire were also increased where incest, illegitimacy, or even a failure to be baptized were involved.

Vampires will never cross water and they are repulsed by fire.

corpse becoming a *vrykolaka*, a wax cross and a fragment of pottery, bearing the inscription, "Jesus Christ Conquers," was placed on the body.

In other parts of Europe corpses might have their tendons severed at the knees to ensure they couldn't climb out of the grave. In other instances, poppy

seeds, sand, or millet would be placed on the ground near to the grave of a suspected vampire, the hope being that the vampire would be too preoccupied, counting the grains all night, to be troublesome. The cairns of prehistoric civilizations were a way of preventing the dead from escaping by placing rocks

on top of the burial site – a method adopted in historical times by people in Ireland. Throughout Europe, as far back as the time of the ancient Romans, there is evidence of suspected vampires, and even criminals, being buried at crossroads, the belief being that in the event of the corpse coming back to life, it would be confused as to the road it should take to return to the place of its original malpractice.

Vampires are repelled by rowan trees and salt, while sunlight destroys them altogether.

LEFT: A vampire is said to leave no reflection in a mirror.

ABOVE: A cross placed outside a house to ward off vampires.

OPPOSITE: Many people took Professor Blomberg's Vampire-Killing Kit seriously, and actually bought one for themselves without realizing it was a joke.

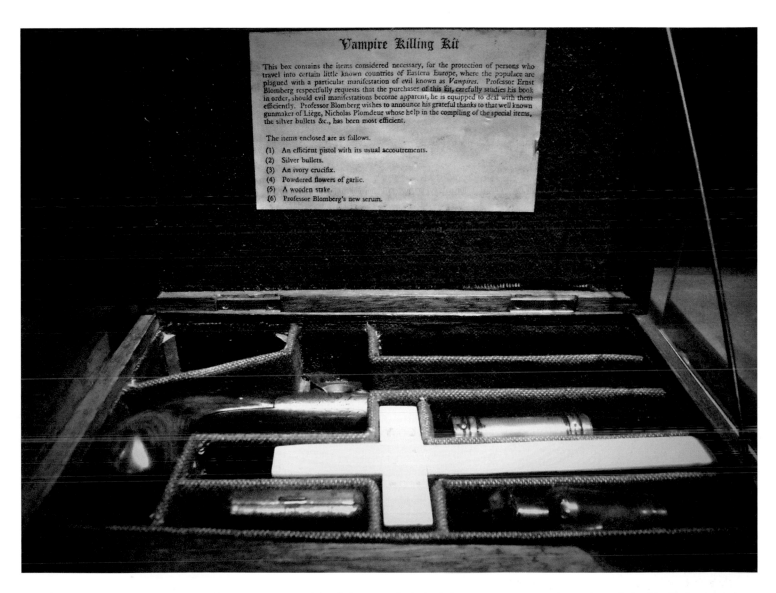

Also common in Europe was the practice of burying suspected vampires with items such as rosary beads or crucifixes, the reason being that such powerful religious symbols had the power to protect the corpse from the attentions of evil spirits or even the devil himself. Many depictions are encountered of a cross being brandished before a vampire in an attempt to drive it away. But the brandisher must be a true believer in the faith for this to be successful.

THE ORIGINS OF VAMPIRES

Seemingly more unusual is the practice of using garlic to ward off vampires. There are many theories as to why this should be efficacious in this task, most of which are fanciful in the extreme. It has been suggested that if the deceased person's mouth is stuffed with garlic, giving it something to chew on, it will dispense with the need to rise up and take human blood. Another, slightly more scientific theory, concerns the connection between vampirism and mosquito bites which, as mentioned earlier, are a means by which the insect obtains its food. Garlic has some insecticidal and antiseptic properties, and

Garlic and garlic flowers are traditional vampire repellents, used for the purpose for over 2,000 years. Garlic oil is also a highly efficient antibiotic.

the suggestion is that its presence may also prevent a vampire from biting to obtain blood.

CHAPTER THREE

VAMPIRES OF THE ANCIENT WORLD

Although in ancient times the term "vampire" itself did not exist, stories of preternatural creatures devouring the blood or flesh of the living have existed in cultures all around the world, and for many hundreds of years. These malevolent activities, however, were attributed to evil spirits and demons; even the devil was implicated in such goings-on and was later deemed to be synonymous with vampires.

LEFT: Persepolis. Belief in bloodsucking demons was once common in ancient Persia, the modern-day Iran.

OPPOSITE LEFT: Detail of "Lilith," from Michelangelo's "Downfall of Adam and Eve and their Expulsion from the Garden of Eden," painted on the Sistine Chapel ceiling.

OPPOSITE RIGHT: Dante Gabriel Rosetti's Lady Lilith (1867).

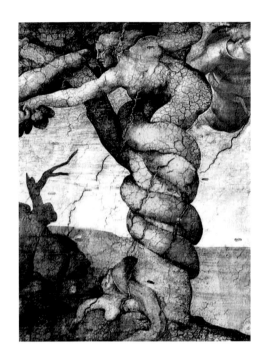

demon with vampiric tendencies was Gallu, who dragged victims away to the Underworld. Among other Mesopotamian demons was the Babylonian goddess Lamashtu, depicted as having a hairy body, the head of a lioness, the ears and teeth of a donkey, and the feet of a bird, complete with sharp talons. It was her habit to menace women during childbirth by watching

Prevalent in the area known as Mesopotamia, which includes modern-day Iraq, was the belief in blood-drinking spirits, while excavated pottery fragments from Persia depict creatures attempting to take blood from men. Ancient Babylonians tell of the mythical Lilitu, a female demon often shown feasting on the blood of babies, and Hebrew mythology has her counterpart, Lilith (*see also* page 33), which prompted mothers to hang amulets from their children's cradles in an attempt to repulse her evil attentions. Another

common one, frequently encountered in the folklore of vampires. The reason often given for this is that the blood of the young is pure and vigorous and thus of greater value.

In India, *vetalas* – vampirelike creatures from Hindu mythology – were said to inhabit corpses. *Vetalas* haunt cemeteries and other burial places, seeking to take demonic possession of the dead. They manifest themselves by tormenting human beings, sometimes driving them mad or causing the deaths of their children. They hang upside down from trees, rather like the bats

them closely before stealing their babies while they were breastfeeding. Then she would suck their blood and chew on their bones. A chronicler describes her as follows: "Wherever she comes, wherever she appears, she brings evil and destruction. Men, beasts, trees, rivers, roads, buildings, she brings harm to them all. A flesh-eating, bloodsucking monster is she."

The association between such demons and their predilection for the blood of children, seems to be a

OPPOSITE: The Hindu god Brahma is said to have created the flesh-eating pishachas.

LEFT: Hindu writings describe the goddess Kali's terrible appearance and association with corpses and war.

BELOW: The Goddess Ambika (here identified with Durga or Chandi) Leading the Eight Matrikas in Battle Against the Demon Raktabija.

associated with vampirism. The way to repel these spirits, trapped as they are in a twilight zone between life and the afterlife, is to chant holy mantras. Other

forms of Hindu demon are the flesh-eating *pishachas* and, although their origins are somewhat obscure, they are believed to have been created by the Hindu god Brahma. *Pishachas* are described as having dark skins and bulging red eyes. They are creatures of the night and lurk in crematoria. Like vampires, they can assume different forms at will, and can even make themselves invisible. They are said to be able to possess human beings, and individuals afflicted in this way may exhibit madness or other maladies. Again, mantras are chanted in an attempt to drive the demons away.

Even the ancient Indian fanged goddess, Kali, depicted surrounded by corpses and skulls, is linked with the drinking of blood, and temples dedicated to her appear to be strategically placed close to crematoria throughout India. One particular story tells how Kali joined in battle with the ten-armed goddess Durga against the demon known as Raktabija. The demon was able to reproduce himself from drops of spilled blood (Raktabija means 'blood-seed'), but Kali drank the blood, ensuring that none

was spilled in the process, and in this way the demon was defeated.

According to myth, the Egyptian god Ra became angry when he saw that mankind was failing to preserve Ma'at (justice or balance). As a punishment, he sent his daughter Hathor to earth in the form of a lion. She became Sekhmet, the "Eye of Ra," and began her rampage, with the result that the fields were soon running with human blood. But the sight of the carnage caused Ra to relent. He ordered Sekhmet to stop, but the bloodlust was upon her and she would not listen. So Ra poured 7,000 jugs of beer and pomegranate juice, which stained the beer blood-red, in her path, leading her to gorge herself on the "blood," which made her so drunk that she slept for three days. When she awoke, her bloodlust had dissipated and humanity was saved.

OPPOSITE: The Egyptian warrior goddess Sekhmet, shown with her sun disk and cobra crown.

RIGHT: Lamia and the Soldier, by John William Waterhouse (1905).

Turning to ancient Greece, we discover the legends of Empusa, the beautiful daughter of the spirit Mormo and the goddess Hecate. Her habit was to seduce men before feasting on their blood while they slept. Later, we find whole species of demons, the Empusae, being ordered by Hecate to lie in wait by roadsides and devour travellers.

The Greeks also tell of the beautiful Lamia, destined to become a child-devouring demon. According to legend, she was the daughter of King Belus of Egypt, and Lamia became queen of Libya, one of her father's territories, when he died. The historian Diodorus relates that Lamia and Zeus had an affair and that Lamia bore children from the union. When Zeus's wife, Hera, discovered this, she killed the children, driving Lamia insane and causing her to devour the children of others, when it is said that her face became distorted and ugly because of her wicked deeds. The legend survives in the personae of the Lamiae – monsters that inhabited caves and dank places and which preyed on young children. They were also reputed to seduce young men before feasting on their blood.

In ancient Rome there was believed to be a creature known as a *strix* (*striges*, to give the plural form). The *strix* was a nocturnal bird and a portent of evil that feasted on human flesh and blood. The name is Greek in origin and means "owl," and *Strix* later became the scientific name for a genus of owl. The connection between the ghostly, nocturnal activities and eerie calls of owls and the demons of mythology can clearly be seen. This, no doubt, also explains why many consider it unlucky to have stuffed owls or any artifacts relating to them displayed in the house. A very early reference to the *strix* comes from the Greek author Boios. He tells of Polyphonte, who was made to fall in love with a bear. Her two half-human sons, Orius and Agrius, were cannibals, and the gods turned them into owl-like creatures.

As well as later Roman references to the *striges*, the legend of the *strix* survived into the Middle Ages and gave rise to the names of imaginary beings in several cultures, including the *striga* (an evil Romanian female) and the s*trega* (an Italian witch).

OPPOSITE: Lamia, a city in central Greece, is reputed to have been named after the mythological Lamia, the daughter of Poseidon and the mother of the sea-monsters Skylla and Akheilos.

RIGHT: Strix aluco, the tawny owl, whose eerie night call has prompted its association with bad luck and death.

CHAPTER FOUR
VAMPIRES IN EUROPE

By the Middle Ages, belief in demons and other such entities, including vampires, was showing no signs of abatement. Indeed, this is often regarded as a period when the creation of yet more myths, surrounding the dark forces, flourished and expanded. At that time, the power of the religious authorities was enormous, second only to that of the monarchy itself. To reinforce this sense of power, and to create a sense of awe in the people in

LEFT: Salisbury Cathedral. To strengthen the power of the Church in the minds of the people, a wave of church-building occurred across Europe in the Middle Ages.

OPPOSITE: Romania is a country with a rich folkloric tradition.

PAGES 88 & 89: St. Michael's Cathedral, built between 1350 and 1487, dominates the old Transylvanian city of Cluj.

general, mighty churches and cathedrals, their spires stretching up to the heavens, began to proliferate.

Because religion, by now, was such a force in the lives of the people, the Church was seen as a bastion against evil and damnation. And what better way to demonstrate the Church's role in society than to have it pitted against adversaries as diverse and menacing as demons, vampires, and their ilk? Thus it could be said that, from the Church's point of view, giving the flock something to fear was a useful means of controlling it. The Greek Church is sometimes accused of promulgating the myth of the vampire for its own purposes, and it is probably true that clergy elsewhere found it provided them with additional power over their congregations.

OPPOSITE: A Greek Orthodox Church. The Greek clergy were often accused of turning the vampire myth to their own advantage.

RIGHT, PAGES 92 & 93: In eastern Europe, graves were often opened to search for evidence of vampire activity.

During the 12th century, the English chroniclers Walter Map and William Newburgh recorded the earliest stories connected with indigenous vampires. At this time, a belief in souls returning from the dead was commonplace, and Newburgh's *Historia* provided brief accounts, including tales of revenants (reanimated corpses).

The tales that were recounted bear a strong resemblance to the folklore that appeared much later in Europe, in the 18th century, and which were the foundations upon which the vampire legends of countries such as England and Germany were built. This was the time when a rash of vampire sightings were being reported in eastern Europe, and coupled with them came stories of all kinds of fervent antivampire activities. Bodies of potential vampires were staked prior to burial in what was regarded as a well-tried safeguard, and bodies were exhumed so that even more stringent measures could be undertaken. The result was that most of Europe was to become engulfed in a frenzy of mass hysteria.

It began in East Prussia with alleged vampire activity in 1721, then spread

to Austria-Hungary and elsewhere from 1725 to 1734. The degree of concern and hysteria that these episodes generated, together with a widespread belief in the existence of vampires and their like, can be illustrated by the examples that follow. They are among the first and most famous of vampire reports, made all the more feasible by the fact that not only did they concern local peasants, who might have been dismissed as uneducated and prone to superstitious beliefs, but also involved the first-hand intervention of state dignitaries, respected surgeons, and the like.

The case of Peter Plogojowitz, a Serbian peasant from the village of Kisilova (then part of Austria), who died in 1725 at the age of 62, illustrates the hysteria gathering pace at the time. Following the death of Plogojowitz, he was in his grave for about three weeks when villagers reported seeing him abroad at night. They claimed he visited them in their beds and attacked them, attempting to suffocate them. Following this, nine villagers died within a week. Even Plogojowitz's wife affirmed that he had visited her after his death and

had asked her for his shoes. In other versions of the tale, Plogojowitz is reported to have returned to his house, after death, and to have callously murdered his own son for refusing to give him food. The villagers of Kisilova then decided to dig up Plogojowitz's body to check for signs of vampirism, insisting that an official, called Frombald, along with the local priest, be present at the disinterment. Frombald advised the villagers that permission for the action should first be sought from the Austrian authorities in Belgrade, but they were reluctant to wait for this to be granted in case the whole village be annihilated by Plogojowitz in the meantime. In the end, faced with threats that the entire village would be abandoned unless permission was granted, Frombald himself reluctantly agreed that the procedure could go ahead.

When the exhumed body was examined, all the indications that Plogojowitz was a vampire were found to be present. The body was not in a state of decomposition, the hair and beard seemed to have grown, and there

was blood in the corpse's mouth. The villagers, accordingly, dragged the body away and proceeded to drive a stake through its heart, causing a great deal of fresh blood to spurt from the ears and mouth. As a final precaution, the body was burned. For his part, Frombald justified his actions on the grounds that the villagers were paralyzed with fear, with the result that the authorities decided not to take further action regarding the incident.

This episode, as one of the first documented accounts of vampirism in eastern Europe, found its way onto the pages of the Viennese newspaper, *Wienerisches Diarium.* Widely translated across northern and western parts of Europe, it helped to fan the flames in countries such as England, Germany, and France. Science, of course, has moved on apace since those times, and the "evidence of vampirism" noted in the exhumed body of Peter Plogojowitz

The strange case of Peter Plogojowitz sent an Austrian village into a paroxysm of fear after he was denounced as a vampire and a spate of sudden deaths were laid at his door.

can be seen as nothing more than the natural processes that occur in a body after death.

Another Serb, by the name of Arnold Paole, not only was a key suspect in an outbreak of vampire activity but is also linked with another that took place within the same region about five years later. Paole was a former militiaman who died in around 1725 or 1726, and who is believed to have become a vampire following his death. It is claimed he was responsible for the deaths of at least 16 people in his village of Meduegna, situated on the Morava river. As was in the case of Peter Plogojowitz, the story surrounding Paole gained prominence due to the involvement of the authorities in Austria and the documentation of the findings by doctors and officials who gave credence to the evidence. The report of their findings found its way to western Europe, where a further spread of interest in vampires was generated.

Arnold Paole had moved to Meduegna from a Turkish-controlled region of Serbia. He is said to have mentioned to people that he had been troubled by a vampire near Gossowa

(possibly Kosovo), but that he had solved the problem by eating soil taken from the grave of the vampire, then burning the body. Paole died following a fall from a wagon, and within 20 or 30 days of his death four people reported having been plagued by him. They all died shortly afterwards.

Ten days later the villagers, encouraged by a military administrator, opened Paole's grave to find similar signs of vampirism that had presented in the Plogojowitz case. Accordingly, a stake was driven through the corpse's

heart, to which it is alleged to have reacted with groans and bleeding. Then the body was burned. Paole's four victims were also disinterred and the same antivampire procedures were performed on their bodies.

The second outbreak occurred during the winter of 1731 when a number of people died within the course of a few weeks, some suddenly and without previously being ill. The number of fatalities vary, but are believed to be between 13 and 17. Two Austrian military doctors, Flückinger and Glaser, one of whom had also reported on the first case involving Arnold Paole some years earlier, were detailed to investigate the case. Glaser's report indicated that the locals considered that two women who had died in the epidemic, one a 50-year-old called Milica and the other a 20-year-old called Stana, had been responsible for the outbreak of vampire

LEFT: The Morava river.

OPPOSITE: Kosovo, in the vicinity of which Arnold Paole was seemingly troubled by a vampire.

activity. Milica had arrived in the village from Ottoman-controlled territories about six years previously, and admitted that while there she had eaten meat from two sheep allegedly killed by vampires. Stana then confessed that while in the same region she had daubed herself with a vampire's blood as a way of protecting herself, vampires being active in the area at the time. In accordance with local beliefs, both of these activities would have been enough to turn the women into vampires after death. The report by Flückinger, which gives the higher figure for the number of victims, also states that Milica had eaten sheep that the previous vampires – in other words, Arnold Paole and his alleged victims of some five years earlier – had killed.

The Austrian military commander responsible for administering the region, fearing an epidemic of plague had broken out, dispatched a specialist in contagious diseases (in this instance, Glaser) to the area to make a report. Glaser examined both the villagers and their houses but could find no signs of disease. Instead, he blamed the deaths on malnutrition and the effects of severe

religious fasting. But the villagers persisted with their claim that the epidemic was the result of vampires. By this time, two or three households were sleeping together for mutual protection and comfort, with some members standing watch while the others slept.

Fearful villagers threatened to abandon their homes en masse if the recently deceased were not exhumed and the "execution" of proven vampires did not take place.

According to the villagers, this dire situation could only be resolved if the authorities destroyed the vampires. Without this assurance, the people threatened abandonment of the village — a strategy that had often, in the past, been deemed necessary in peasant cultures when a community had been visited by severe troubles that seemed otherwise insurmountable.

Eventually, therefore, to calm the villagers' fears and prevent the threatened exodus, Glaser agreed to exhume some of the victims of the outbreak to ascertain what, if any, vampiric evidence could be uncovered. To his astonishment he found that many of the bodies had not decomposed at all, but were swollen and showed traces of blood around the mouths. To compound matters further, several other people, who had died earlier than the ones displaying the vampiric signs, were in an advanced state of decomposition, which was to be expected if nothing untoward had been taking place. Glaser's report to his superiors came with the recommendation that the worried villagers should indeed be permitted to "execute" these proven vampires, so that the matter could be resolved once and for all. The report then found its way to the supreme command in Belgrade itself, whence the vice commandant, Botta d'Adorno, dispatched another commission to look into the case.

This new commission included the military surgeon Flückinger, several other surgeons, military officers, and other officials. Thus it was that on July 7, accompanied by the village dignitaries and some local gypsies, the deceased were once again exhumed. What they discovered concurred with Glaser's findings, and they too documented the case in even more detail than had previously been the case. The report concluded that although five of the deceased were showing the expected signs of decomposition consistent with a normal death and burial, no fewer than 12 of the corpses were "quite complete and undecayed," thus displaying all the

hallmarks of vampirism. For example, their chests and even some of their internal organs were found to be filled with fresh, rather than coagulated, blood; the skin, instead of being pallid, was said to be red and vivid; the corpses looked plump and not wasted; some even showed signs of growing new nails and skin. The report on the examination of Milica stated that she was found to be in a plump condition, whereas in life she had always been "very lean and dried-up."

In summary, it was concluded that the corpses thus described were in a vampiric condition and, following the examinations, the gypsies were permitted to cut the heads from the bodies before burning both the heads and bodies and scattering the ashes in the Morava river. The bodies that had shown signs of decomposition, and were therefore beyond suspicion, were again laid to rest in the ground. Doctor Johann Friedrich Glaser, a Viennese physician and the father of one of the investigating surgeons, sent a letter to

People were terrified of what they feared might inhabit the night.

the Nuremberg journal *Commercium Litterarium* in which he described the cases as told to him by his son. The more detailed report of the incident, as conducted by Flückinger, was also widely disseminated at the time.

Another case of vampirism that aroused much interest at the time was that of the Serbian Sava Savanovic. It is said that he lived in a watermill on the Rogacica river in the western mountains of Serbia, and that it was his habit to drink the blood of millers who came to use his watermill to grind their corn. The mill remained in the hands of the Yagodith family for several decades until the 1950s, when it was shut down, although it still attracts a few curious tourists.

The legend of the vampire miller found fame in 1973 when the film *Leptirica* ("The Butterfly") was released, based on the story, "After Ninety Years," by the Serbian Milovan Glisic. The

Bodies that showed signs of normal decomposition, and which were therefore beyond suspicion, were again laid to rest in their graves.

opening scenes show an old miller being bitten while he sleeps by a humanlike creature with long teeth and black hands. Later, a young man, Strahinya, denied in his amorous pursuit of Radojka, the daughter of a wealthy landowner, takes up the offer to become the miller in that same remote mill. During the night he survives an attack by a creature, discovering its name is Sava Savanovic. The villagers, fearful that a vampire is abroad, discover that there is a grave of someone with that very name nearby. Finding it, they drive a stake through the coffin, releasing a butterfly from it in the process.

The villagers then help Strahinya to abduct Radojka and take her to the mill to prepare for their wedding. During the night, however, Strahinya goes to his betrothed's room and undresses her. To his alarm, he discovers a bloody hole beneath her breast. At this, Radojka opens her eyes and is transformed into a hideous creature that attempts to bite

The hysteria that surrounded these so-called vampiric episodes persisted in communities for many years.

Strahinya on the neck. Eventually, at the grave of Sava Savanovic, Strahinya manages to remove the stake from the body and drive it into the heart of Radojka, following which a butterfly is seen fluttering around Strahinya's head.

The widespread interest caused by well-reported cases, such as that of Arnold Paole, and fueled by the intervention of some well-respected people who became involved in the investigations, caused a state of general hysteria to prevail for many years. Nor was this hysteria calmed by the continuing reports of rural epidemics of vampirism coming to light and the associated "remedies" to which the corpses were subjected. Of course, not everyone either believed in such creatures or even had sympathy for those who did, although several learned scholars tried, without much success, to shed the light of reason on the phenomenon.

The French theologian Dom Antoine Augustin Calmet who died in 1757, was a Benedictine monk who wrote several treatises and other important works. In 1746, his *Treatise on the Vampires of Hungary and the Surrounding*

Regions or The Phantomic World was published, in which the possibility of vampires was explored, and which included many reports of vampiric incidents. But his work was ambiguous to say the least, and he never stated explicitly what his feelings on the subject

actually were. Calmet's work even prompted the respected writer and philosopher, Voltaire, to comment on the subject, and Voltaire mentions the phenomenon in one of his own works, the *Dictionnaire Philosophique (Philosophical Dictionary)*, published in 1764.

Ending the Hysteria

Eventually, in an attempt to call a halt to the hysteria once and for all, Empress Maria Theresa of Austria ordered her personal doctor, the Dutch-Austrian Gerard van Swieten, to investigate the phenomenon. Van Swieten was to become an important figure in the furor because of the part he played in the battle against superstition during the 18th-century Age of Enlightenment, and especially that which pertained to the vampires reported in eastern European villages from about 1718 to 1732. He considered the belief to be nothing more than a "barbarism of ignorance," and set out on a campaign to eradicate it. So began a thorough investigation culminating in his report, "Abhandlung des Daseyns der Gespenster" (Discourse

OPPOSITE: The hysteria surrounding the vampire myth prompted Voltaire to comment on the phenomenon in 1764.

RIGHT: The Empress Maria Theresa of Austria ordered an investigation so that the hysteria surrounding vampirism could be brought to a halt.

proposed that much of the phenomenon was simply the result of fear, superstition, an overactive imagination, and ignorance. Later, other physicians corroborated his views by suggesting that it may simply have been epidemics of contagious diseases that had been responsible for the deaths. As a result of Gerard van Swieten's findings, the empress decreed that all traditional methods of vampire destruction, such as impaling, beheading, and the burning of bodies, were henceforth to be prohibited. Although the edict brought an end to the immediate hysteria, tales of the undead continued to live on in local folklore and mythology, and were later to be perpetuated in various artistic works.

Vampires in Britain

Anyone acquainted with Bram Stoker's *Dracula* will be aware that not all of the action takes place in the wild, remote lands of Transylvania; in fact, a crucial part of the story is set in Whitby, in Yorkshire, in the north of England. Such is the power of Stoker's novel that, over 100 years later, the town has maintained

on the Existence of Ghosts), in which he proposed an explanation for the belief in vampires based entirely on natural, rather than supernatural, events.

Van Swieten attributed the suspicious appearance of some of the exhumed corpses to plausible processes, such as fermentation preventing the onset of decomposition. He further

FAR LEFT: Gerard van Swieten, whose investigations put an end to vampire hysteria in Austria.

BELOW: Bram Stoker brought the vampire legend to Britain by setting parts of his Dracula novel in Whitby, a town in north-east England.

OPPOSITE: The fishing town of Whitby.

PAGE 108: Bram Stoker's house in London.

PAGES 108–109: Historic Whitby is situated in the Scarborough district of Yorkshire.

its reputation for dark and mysterious goings-on. Dracula apart, incidences of vampirism in England are few and far between. There is, however, the well-documented 12th-century case of a deceased man in Buckingham, who is said to have appeared before his wife and other relatives on several occasions at night. In the end, the Bishop of Lincoln reluctantly agreed to have the corpse burned, and it was duly disinterred so that an exorcism could first be performed. On exhuming the body, it was found to be as fresh as if death had occurred on the previous day.

Thereafter, the nightly appearances of the revenant ceased.

In rather more modern times, vampire activity is alleged to have occurred in Highgate Cemetery in north London, following which the supposed entity not surprisingly became known as the Highgate Vampire, with interest in it lasting for decades. Of all the places that could be described as the ideal setting for such paranormal events, Highgate Cemetery would probably be near to the top of the list. Opened in 1839, this large and rambling burial ground, set on a wooded hillside, was designed as part of a system of seven large cemeteries created around London and designed to help cope with the number of burials required in a large city, which local churchyards were finding themselves unable to accommodate.

Because of the Victorian attitude to death, loved ones erected great numbers of Gothic-style tombs, mausoleums and

OPPOSITE: *Whitby Abbey, built on the east cliff overlooking the Esk River and town of Whitby, was the site of the Synod of Whitby, at which the Northumbrian Celtic church was reconciled with Rome.*

RIGHT: *Brams Stoker's portrait of a vampire as an aristocrat is repeated in various imagery.*

memorials in memory of the departed, often set among sheltering trees. (In fact, Highgate Cemetery contains the finest collection of Victorian funerary architecture in England, and is today a regularly visited tourist attraction.) The site occupies an area of 37 acres (15 hectares) and is the final resting place of 165,000 souls. Among the many famous people buried here are the pioneering scientist Michael Faraday, the

communist revolutionary Karl Marx, and the Victorian novelist George Eliot. The entire place is one of overgrown gloom, and the many trees, shrubs, and decaying, ivy-clad tombstones, together with the undulating site, adds to its sense of mystery, inaccessibility and downright spookiness. In fact, Bram Stoker is reputed to have been inspired to write *Dracula* by the eerie atmosphere that pervaded the cemetery.

In 1963, two convent schoolgirls, walking past the cemetery's north gate, claimed to have seen bodies emerging from tombs. Highgate Cemetery had become extremely dilapidated and overgrown around this time, with many of the graves suffering the effects of neglect, the place having often been subjected to vandalism by intruders. There were even grizzly reports of

Highgate Cemetery, designated Grade II* on the English Heritage Register of Parks and Gardens of Special Historic Interest.
In the 1960s and '70s stories of vampire activity and satanic ritual connected with the place were proliferating fast. Could it be true that the undead inhabit this place?

LEFT & OPPOSITE: Highgate Cemetery is the final resting place of famous people such as Michael Faraday, Karl Marx and George Eliot. Its eerie atmosphere may well have influenced Bram Stoker when writing his novel Dracula.

corpses being removed from coffins at night and macabre dances being performed with them, while rumors also circulated of satanic rituals taking place.

Also in the 1960s, a group of young people with an interest in the occult began to frequent the cemetery, one of whom was David Farrant, the president of the British Psychic and Occult Society. In December 1969 he claims to have glimpsed a figure in the cemetery that he did not consider to be human. Following enquiries as to whether other people had seen anything similar, various eyewitnesses came forward to tell of their own sightings of supernatural figures in the vicinity. As is often the case in such instances, the accounts were lurid and varied, and included ghosts on bicycles, figures wading in a pond, and a face seen gazing through the bars of a gate.

The events were also brought to the attention of Seán Manchester, a priest and mystic, who was as keen as Farrant to identify and then eliminate what he thought might be an evil entity at large. In February 1970, a local newspaper, the *Hampstead and Highgate Express,* reported that Manchester believed that "a King Vampire of the Undead" had been brought to England from Wallachia in the early 18th century, and that it had been buried in ground now forming part of Highgate Cemetery. (Manchester later remarked that this was a mere journalistic embellishment, although in the 1985 edition of his book he speaks of an unnamed nobleman's body having been brought to Highgate in a coffin from somewhere in Europe.) It was also reported that satanists were attempting to rouse the vampire from its grave. Manchester suggested, therefore, that the body be exhumed, staked, and beheaded, and the head burned; it is not surprising, however, that this drastic solution failed to be popular with the authorities, and the *Hampstead and Highgate Express* was prompted to ask: "Does a Vampyr Walk in Highgate?"

Soon afterwards, both Manchester and Farrant reported seeing dead foxes in the cemetery bearing throat wounds, and which had been drained of their blood. It isn't clear why a rampant vampire should have chosen the blood of animals when there were so many human victims in the vicinity, but neither Manchester nor Farrant chose to challenge the discoveries, with both seemingly content to lay the blame at the door of an active vampire rather than assume that an elaborate hoax had been perpetrated. A fierce rivalry developed between the two, with both claiming to have seen the Highgate Vampire, and with each equally desirous of eliminating the evil being. Manchester then decided to hold an official vampire hunt on Friday, March 13, 1970, and both Manchester and Farrant gave televised interviews, together with others claiming to have witnessed strange occurrences. Soon after the interviews had been broadcasted, scores of people from all over London descended on the cemetery, despite the efforts of police to keep unauthorized vampire-hunters out.

OPPOSITE & BELOW: Highgate Cemetery, being gloomy, overgrown, and somewhat neglected, is undoubtedly an eerie place; in fact it is the very place where overactive imaginations would tend to run riot.

In his book *The Highgate Vampire,* Manchester recalls his own activities that night, telling how, unbeknown to the police, he and several companions entered the cemetery, then attempted to open up a particular catacomb to which a psychic sleepwalker had led him. Its door wouldn't open, and so they eventually managed to climb down inside through a hole in the roof, using a rope.

Inside, they found several empty coffins into which they placed some garlic, also sprinkling holy water around. A few months later, the charred remains of a headless woman were found near the catacomb, leading police to suspect that a black magic ritual had taken place. Then, one night, Farrant was discovered

in the churchyard next to the cemetery bearing a crucifix and a wooden stake. He was arrested, but the case was later dismissed.

On a later daytime visit to Highgate Cemetery, Manchester claims that he and his associates managed to force open the doors to a family vault and discovered a coffin, which he believed had been lying in the catacomb he had entered on a previous occasion. His intention was to drive a stake through the body in the coffin, but his companions dissuaded him. Three years later, he claimed to have found a vampiric corpse in the cellar of an empty house in the Highgate area (he implies it was the same body), and that this time he did indeed stake the body before burning it.

In 1974 Farrant was tried and jailed for five years for desecrating memorials and interfering with corpses at Highgate Cemetery, although he claims it was not him but the work of satanists. Another investigator, an American specialist in satanism in modern culture, Professor Bill Ellis, wrote a learned account of the vampiric activities at Highgate in the publication, *Folklore*.

Despite the strong media and public interest in the case of the Highgate Vampire, there remains tantalizingly little by way of solid evidence to support the view that Highgate Cemetery was the site of vampiric activity, or indeed of any other paranormal occurrences. The alleged discoveries made by those investigating the phenomenon had been achieved without any independent witnesses or media agencies being present to corroborate their findings. Moreover, others with an interest in vampirism have challenged many of the Highgate vampire-hunters' claims and findings. It seems, therefore, that the search for irrefutable physical proof of the existence of vampires is destined to continue.

OPPOSITE: It would appear that the ability of the human race to believe in vampires, even in modern times, is a strongly persistent one.

RIGHT: The grave of Karl Marx, a German philosopher, political economist, historian, political theorist, sociologist, communist, and revolutionary, whose ideas became the foundation of modern communism.

CHAPTER FIVE
VAMPIRES IN AMERICA & THE CARIBBEAN

A creature, known as the *loogaroo*, and which exists in Caribbean mythology, is said to be akin to a vampire, and is also reputed to be a woman in league with the devil. She retains her magical powers only as long as she provides the devil with blood each night. She therefore attempts to get blood from other victims, believing she will surely die if the devil takes blood only from her own body. Each night, the *loogaroo* leaves her skin under a silk-cotton (kapok) tree before transforming herself into a ball of flame or bright-blue light that searches out victims to provide the blood she needs. Once enough has been collected, she is free to

RIGHT: Each night, the loogaroo sheds her skin, leaving it behind under a kapok tree.

OPPOSITE: The Caribbean has more than its fair share of vampire legends.

revert to her human form. Locals attempt to divert the *loogaroo* from her evil intentions by spreading rice near to the doors of their houses. This is said to stop the *loogaroo* in her tracks, for she will be unable to resist the compulsion to count the rice, grain by grain; the hope is that she will take so long that the sun will have risen before she has finished her task, and she will have regained her human form. *Loogaroo* is possibly a corruption of the French word for a mythological creature, known as the *loup-garou*, a type of werewolf. The *loogaroo* is also known in the state of Louisiana in the United States.

A similar creature, known as the *soucouyant* or *soucriant*, exists in the folklore of Trinidad and Guadeloupe. By day, the *soucouyant* takes the form of an old woman, but as night falls, she abandons her skin and assumes the form of a fireball, flying through the darkness, looking for victims whose blood she can

OPPOSITE & RIGHT: Guadeloupe and Trinidad share the folklore of the soucouyant, an old woman transformed into a bloodsucking fireball by night.

suck. The fireball is able to enter houses through even the smallest crevice or keyhole. If a *soucouyant* takes too much blood, then it is believed that the victim will die, following which they will become a *soucouyant* themselves. *Soucouyants* belong to a group of spirits known as *jumbies*, which are especially prevalent in English-speaking Caribbean states that were colonized by the British, and which came to practice a form of sorcery, known as obeah, which combines traditional African beliefs with Christian notions concerning death.

It is said that a female monster, La Tunda, frequents the Colombian Pacific region, luring the unsuspecting into forests with the intention of draining their blood. La Tunda's shape-shifting abilities are far from perfect, however, for whatever form she assumes will invariably have a wooden leg in the

The Colombian Pacific coast is where La Tundra, another vampire monster, lures her victims into forests with the intention of draining their blood from their bodies.

shape of a *molinillo* (wooden kitchen utensil). The monster, however, is very cunning, and is adept at concealing this defect from would-be victims.

There is a creature known as the *peuchen* in the Mapuche and Chilote mythology of southern Chile. This shape-shifting entity may appear as any animal, but particularly as a huge flying snake that can paralyze with a glance in order to suck a victim's blood. Only a *machi* – a medicine woman – has the power to eliminate the creature. In Mexico, the *civateteo* are the spirits of women who died in childbirth. They are guilty of making all kinds of mischief, attacking children and even of seducing human men.

The Chilean peuchen *shape-shifts into a flying snake to feed on human blood.*

New England, in the United States, particularly Rhode Island and Connecticut, has long had associations with vampires, especially during the late-18th and 19th centuries. This was when the then imperfectly understood disease,

known as "consumption" but which we now know to be pulmonary tuberculosis, was prevalent. There were instances of loved ones exhuming the bodies of their deceased in order to remove their hearts, in the common belief that, as vampires, they were bringing sickness or death to the living family. In the so-called consumptive state, the victim becomes very pale, stops eating, and literally wastes away. At night, the condition worsens, and fluid and blood may collect in the lungs. During the later stages of the disease, blood may be seen on the patient's face, neck, and nightclothes,

breathing is laborious, and the body becomes starved of oxygen.

Perhaps it is New England's strong and long-standing historical connections with old European cultures that has fostered the myths of vampires and other supernatural occurrences in the area; for example, much of the action in the novel *Salem's Lot* occurs in the state of Maine.

The case of Mercy Brown amply demonstrates the superstitions that surrounded suspected vampirism as recently as the 1890s in the United States. Towards the end of the 19th century, in the town of Exeter, Rhode Island, a family by the name of Brown fell victim to the ravages of the much-dreaded consumption. The first victim was Mary, the mother of the family. Then, in 1888, Mary Olive, the eldest daughter, also succumbed to the disease and died. The son, Edwin, contracted the disease in 1890, and as if this was not tragic enough, yet another daughter, Mercy, died in January 1892.

As mentioned earlier, the true causes of consumption were little understood at the time, but to superstitious locals the incidence of so many deaths in a single family could mean only one thing: vampirism. Therefore, and in accordance with tradition, the only way to get to the truth of the matter was to exhume the bodies to find evidence of undead activity. The father of the family, George Brown, eventually was persuaded to open his family's coffins, and this he did with the aid of several other villagers on March 17, 1892. When the bodies were examined, it was discovered that the corpses of Mary and Mary Olive, which had been in the ground for several years, were in a state of advanced decomposition. Mercy's body, however, having been laid to rest relatively recently, was found to be in good condition and still had blood in the heart. These discoveries were taken to be clear evidence that 19-year-old Mercy was the vampire in question.

What had not been apparent to the fearful villagers, however, was that the cold New England winter, during which Mercy's death had occurred, had prevented her body from being committed to the rock-hard soil, and it had been laid in a crypt above ground in

Exeter's Baptist church, where the freezing conditions helped to keep the body in almost perfect condition. Despite this, Mercy's heart was cut from her body and burned, the remains mixed with water and given to Edwin to drink, in the vain hope that he would be protected from further harm. But the remedy proved ineffective, and Edwin died only two months later.

OPPOSITE & ABOVE: Exeter, Rhode Island's cemetery and Baptist Church. Mercy Brown, having been declared a vampire, was buried here after her body was exhumed and her heart cut out and burned.

Asian traditions of vampires have their origins in ancient folklore, with many legends of ghoulish entities coming from both the islands and the mainland of this huge continent. India has several such legends, one of which concerns the *bhutas*. In Sanskrit, the word *bhuta* has several meanings, but its most macabre form describes the ghost or spirit of a dead person, especially one who has suffered an untimely death, was insane, or was born deformed. *Bhutas* are said to wander the night, appearing as dark shadows, flickering lights or misty apparitions, sometimes entering corpses and leading them, in their ghoulish state, to devour living persons. The *brahmaparusha* is a similar entity known in northern India, while another fierce creature is the *baital*, a short, half-human, half-batlike creature.

The Indian vampires, known as the *pacu pati*, are regarded as the epitome of evil, having begun life as normal

children until the onset of puberty, when they begin to feed on negative energy, such as fear, sorrow, anger, hatred, jealousy, etc., appearing at night in graveyards and at places of execution. These flesh-eating creatures are believed to have been created because of the wrongdoings of mankind.

Another creature, the *churail*, is thought to be the spirit of a woman who has died during the Diwali festival. She preys upon young men,

holding them captive while their life force is drained from their bodies and they become old and withered. The spirit of Indian burial grounds is called the *masani*. This female vampire hunts at night, after emerging from a funeral pyre. The *rakshasa* appears as a human being with animal features, such as fangs and claws, or as an animal with human features, such as hands. It devours the flesh of its victim and drinks its blood.

The *nukekubi* are Japanese monsters, the name coming from the word for "detachable neck" and, as will be explained shortly, describes how the creatures go about their dire business.

ABOVE LEFT: The rakshasa is half-human, half-animal.

RIGHT: Bhutas wander the night, appearing as shadows or misty apparitions.

BELOW: The penanggalan is an extremely unpleasant entity which seeks out the vulnerable, such as women in childbirth.

reunited with the bodies before sunrise, otherwise the creatures will perish. During the time heads and necks are detached to go about their dreadful business, the bodies becomes lifeless. In some legends, it is said that would-be victims have discovered the headless

During the day, *nukekubi* give the impression of being normal human beings, which allows them to infiltrate human society. The tell-tale signs that they are not at all normal, in fact, are the lines of red marks surrounding their necks, which they attempt to disguise by wearing scarves, thick necklaces and other devices. When night falls,

however, their true nature becomes apparent. For now their heads and necks detach themselves from their bodies, which then fly through the air in search of human prey. A victim is first frightened, then mesmerized by the piercing screams emitted by the head, following which the monster closes in and delivers a bite.

But the *nukekubi* have one real weakness: the heads and necks must be

bodies of *nukekubi*, and have either destroyed them or hidden them away, thus causing the creatures' demise.

In the folklore of parts of South-East Asia, such as Malaysia, Indonesia, and the Philippines, vampirelike creatures with similar head-detaching abilities are also encountered. The *penanggalan* (the word means "detach" or "remove") is a vampire that appears to have originated in the Malay Peninsula. It is a detached female head, armed with fangs that, like its Japananese counterpart, is able to fly freely about. As it does so, the creature's stomach and entrails dangle beneath it, flashing like fireflies in the night. Again, illustrating the similarity with the *nukekubi*, the *penanggalan* appears to exist by day, or when not in its "detached" state, as a normal person.

The Malay Peninsula, as well as other parts of South-East Asia, is the home of the penanggalan.

According to Malaysian folklore, a *penanggalan* is a beautiful woman, usually a midwife, who has obtained her good looks through the powers of black magic or other supernatural forces. Occasionally, however, a woman may

have become a *penanggalan* due to a strong curse having been placed upon her or as the result of some kind of demonic possession. In any event, the woman has broken a promise not to eat meat for 40 days, and because of this she is doomed to become a bloodsucking vampire for all eternity.

She keeps a vat of vinegar in her house she uses to shrink her entrails after her nightly hunting expeditions so that they will fit back into her body. A slight variation on this tale has it that the *penanggalan* was a beautiful woman who was bathing in a tub that once contained vinegar, when a man entered the room. This startled her greatly, causing her to jerk her head upwards with such force that it severed her head from her body, dragging her entrails out in the process. In a fit of rage, the head flew at the man, dragging its entrails behind it while the rest of the body languished in the tub. This also explains why, in this version of the legend, the *penanggalan* always emits the smell of vinegar, which is one of the ways the creature can be distinguished from a normal woman.

The *penanggalan* usually seeks out vulnerable people, such as young children or pregnant women. She crouches on the roofs of houses when women are in labor, emitting a screeching sound when the child is born. Then, the ghastly creature inserts her long, invisible tongue into the house to lap up the blood of the new mother, following which the mother becomes afflicted with a wasting disease that is

nearly always fatal. Even if a person does not suffer through having its blood drained by the *penanggalan*, they will suffer painful running sores as a result should they inadvertantly touch the creature's dripping entrails. The *penanggalan*'s insidious powers seem to know no bounds: some claim she can pass with ease through walls or even seep through floorboards, rising up into the room where a victim may be

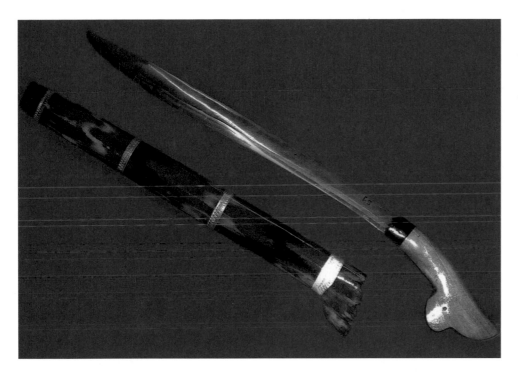

sleeping. It is also claimed that the penanggalan is able to wave her entrails about like tentacles.

It is not unusual, when encountering tales and myths of evil spirits, also to discover the ways in which local people try to protect themselves from attack. In the case of the penanggalan, the most common method is to scatter the thorny leaves of a plant of the Pandanus genus (sometimes known as the screwpine) about, or alternatively hang them around the windows. The belief is that the leaves will snag the entrails of the creature as it flies about looking for prey. To prevent the penanggalan from coming up through the floorboards, prickly plants, such as pineapples, are sometimes placed beneath the house before a woman is due to give birth. A trapped penanggalan may also be killed with a machete or machetelike tool called a parang. Some pregnant women keep scissors or betel-nut cutters beneath their pillows, since the penanggalan has a particular fear of these items.

Although it is difficult to distinguish a penanggalan from a normal person, there are one or two pointers towards recognition: a penanggalan is said to avoid eye contact when meeting people and will also lick her lips while performing her duties as a midwife – no doubt in anticipation of the blood feast she will enjoy later on. And if the place where a penanggalan lives can be discovered, it is sometimes possible for a brave person to wait until the head and entrails have flown off before pouring broken glass into the empty neck cavity. Alternatively, the body, once detached from its head and trailing organs, can be burned; even turning the body over can be beneficial, for when the head reattaches it will do so back to front, revealing the creature's true identity to one and all.

OPPOSITE & BELOW: In folklore, Rangda, the queen of the leyaks, is a cannibalistic demon. Rangda masks are used in Balinese temple death festivals.

Another being, consisting of a fanged, flying head trailing entrails, known as the *leyak*, is said to exist in Bali. *Leyaks* are human beings with cannibalistic instincts that indulge in

black magic. The queen of the *leyaks* is a widow-witch by the name of Rangda, and a mask bearing her image is paraded during temple death festivals. Legend has it that *leyaks* feed on corpses using their

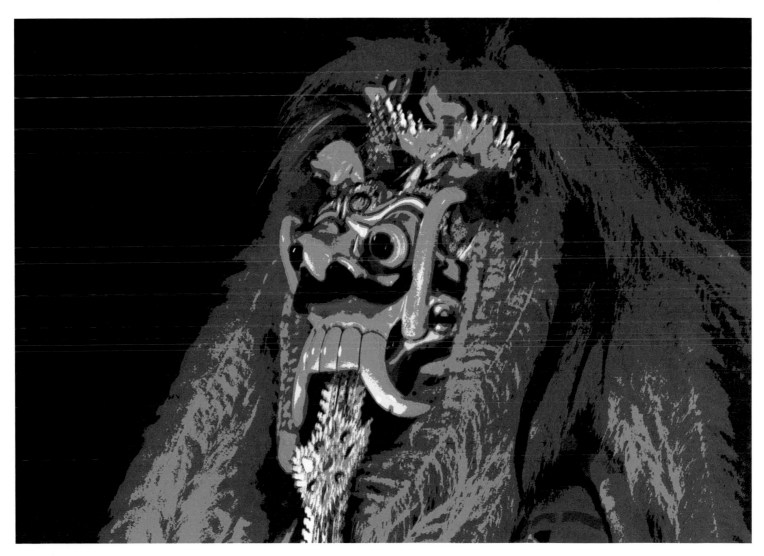

fangs and long tongues, and that they have the power to change themselves into animals; they can, of course, also fly. *Leyaks* are important icons in Balinese culture, and statues of them are sometimes hung on the walls of houses for decorative purposes. A horror movie revolving around the myth of the *leyak*, and entitled *Mystics in Bali,* was released in 1981, and gained cult status around the world.

In both Malaysia and Indonesia there is said to exist an entity that was once a woman who died in childbirth to subsequently become one of the undead. She now seeks revenge and spends her time terrorizing villages. Indonesians call this spirit the *matianak*, while in Malaysia it is known as the *pontianak*. Its form is that of a beautiful young woman, in

LEFT: The matianak or pontianak lives in a banana tree by day, seeking out and attacking her victims by night.

OPPOSITE: The manananggal's lower torso is vulnerable when separated from the upper torso, and applying salt and garlic to the lower torso will prevent the two from reuniting.

order to attract its victims, which are usually young men. The creature lives in a banana tree by day, at night killing its victims by gouging into their bodies with its sharp fingernails so that it can feast on their organs. It is only by doing this that it can survive. It is thought that the *pontianak* finds its prey by detecting their smell on clothes left outside to dry; because of this, many Malays will not leave clothes outside their houses at night. The Malay spirit, known as the *langsuir*, gains possession of a victim, then sucks their blood from the inside, gradually causing their death. It is depicted as a hideous creature with

sharp claws, an evil face, long fangs, and long hair.

In the Philippines the Tagalog people – a large ethnic group consisting of about 28 per cent of the total Filipino population – tell of the vampirelike *mandurugo*. The creature assumes the form of a pretty girl during the day, but as night falls she develops wings and a long, thin, hollow tongue that she uses to suck the blood of her victims. In the myths of another ethnic group of Filipinos, the Visayans, the *manananggal* is described as a beautiful, mature woman who is able to sever her upper torso from the rest of her body in order to fly by night on huge, batlike wings to prey on sleeping pregnant women. Using her long tongue, which resembles an insect's proboscis, the

manananggal drains the victim's blood and may even suck out the heart of the unborn fetus.

Thus the similarities between the body-separating methods of the *manananggal* and those of creatures such as the Japanese *nukekubi* and Balinese *leyaks* are quite noticeable. There is also a similarity in the strategy used for bringing about the creature's demise, for when the *manananggal* is going about its nightly business, the torso that remains behind is vulnerable and can readily be destroyed. It is thought that sprinkling salt or smearing cloves of crushed garlic over the lower torso may also be effective in preventing the upper part of the creature's body from reuniting with its lower half. To this day, superstitious Visayans hang cloves of garlic or onions around their windows to prevent *manananggals* from entering.

Jiang shi, sometimes called Chinese vampires by Westerners, are reanimated corpses that are reputed to hop around, killing living creatures in order to obtain their life essence. The mythology of the *jiang shi* (the words mean "stiff corpse") tells how the creatures are created when

OPPOSITE: Visayans hang strings of onions and garlic around their windows to deter manananggals from entering their houses.

BELOW: Bamboo rods, being flexible, caused corpses, when carried on them, to bounce up and down, which may explain the strange hopping gait jiang shi adopt as they move along.

souls fail to leave the bodies of the dead. This may happen for several reasons: the funeral may not have been conducted according to the proper rites; the burial was in some other way conducted in an inappropriate manner; or the death may be the result of suicide. Sometimes, however, it appears that the creatures are simply out to cause trouble. The outward appearances of *jiang shi* are variable, sometimes resembling the recently deceased, at other times being even more abhorrent, their rotting flesh reminiscent of a corpse that has been dead for some time. A greenish-white, furry covering is usually seen on the skin, which is attributed to mold growing on what is left of the flesh.

So where did the legend of the *jiang shi* originate? Many sources are possible as a result of the Chinese practice of travelling huge distances in a vast country in search of work. If someone were to die on one of these lengthy expeditions, it is unlikely that family and friends back home would have been able to afford a wagon to carry the deceased back to their village for a proper burial. Therefore, the bereaved would have often hired Taoist priests to transport the dead, who would carry the corpse only at night and ringing bells to announce their presence, since it was considered bad luck to set eyes on the dead. Corpses would often be carried on bamboo rods or poles, and because the bamboo was flexible, moving up and down as the bearers walked along, the corpses appeared to be bouncing or hopping, explaining the unusual way of moving attributed to the *jiang shi*.

CHAPTER SEVEN
VAMPIRES IN AFRICA

There are other parts of the world that have vampiric traditions. In Africa, the Ashanti people of Ghana, Côte d'Ivoire, and Togo, in West Africa, tell of the *asanbosam*, a tree-dwelling entity said to be armed with iron teeth and to have iron hooks instead of feet. Its high vantage point allows it to watch and wait, ready to attack travellers as they come into view.

The Ewe people of the south-eastern corner of Ghana, Togo, and

witch, and can then make their own victims poor, using the powers of the *adze*. The *adze* is a dangerous creature, even when not channelling its powers through a witch, for it can pass through closed doors and suck blood from the thumbs of people as they sleep, following

Benin fear a vampire known as the *adze*. It assumes the form of a firefly, although it can also take on human form if captured. The *adze* is said to be able to possess people at will, and a victim so possessed is thought subsequently to become a

The Ewe people of West Africa live in fear of a vampire known as the adze, *which appears as a firefly but can assume human form if captured.*

which the victim will fall ill and die. It is interesting to note that the Ewe characterize the *adze* as a firefly, since another small nocturnal insect, the mosquito, does indeed suck the blood of human victims, frequently transmitting to them a deadly disease known as malaria.

In the eastern Cape region, a creature known as the *impundulu* figures largely in the myths and beliefs of southern African tribes, such as the Xhosa and Zulu. The word means "lightning bird," and the creature takes the form of a black-and-white bird of human size that is said to use its wings and talons to summon up thunder. It has vampiric instincts, and is associated with witchcraft in that it is the servant of a witch or a witch doctor, and attacks their enemies. The *impundulu* itself has an insatiable appetite for blood.

In Madagascar, the Betsileo people tell of the vampirelike *ramanga*, which evolved from a race of servants forced to eat the nail parings and drink any blood lost by their masters. In the event of a master cutting himself or being

wounded in battle, the *ramanga* would lick the wounds, restoring his master to full health.

Southern African tribes, such as the Zulu, believe in the existence of the impundulu *or vampiric lightning bird.*

CHAPTER EIGHT
VLAD TEPES

No account of vampires would be complete without a trip back to the 15th century to meet one of the most notorious and ruthless rulers of the period. Vlad III of Wallachia, otherwise Vlad Dracula, was no character of myth and legend but a true-life despot. He was more chillingly known as Vlad Tepes, the word *tepes* meaning "impaler," and the epithet became attached to his name due to his sadistic method of dealing with his enemies, of which more will be said later. But let us look at the background of this tyrant.

The origin of the name "Dracula" can be traced back to the reign of King Sigismund of Hungary, who became Holy Roman Emperor in 1410. Under his rule, a group of knights, known as the Order of the Dragon, was established with the purpose of defending the realm against the

Ottoman Turks, the emblem of the order being a cross bearing a winged dragon. The father of Vlad III, Vlad II, was inducted into the order and subsequently wore the emblem as ruler of Wallachia (a part of present-day southern Romania). The Romanian word for dragon is *dracul*, so Vlad II became known as Vlad Dracul, meaning "Vlad the Dragon." It follows, therefore, that his son, Vlad III, would become known as Vlad Draculea or Dracula, the "Son of the Dragon."

LEFT: Vlad III of Wallachia.

OPPOSITE LEFT: A portrait of Oswald von Wolkenstein, a diplomat in the service of King Sigismund, wearing the Order of the Dragon, 1432.

OPPOSITE RIGHT: Sigismund, Holy Roman Emperor and King of Hungary.

The Battle for the Throne

Vlad III was born in 1431 in Sighisoara in Transylvania. As he grew, he received scholarly instruction and was tutored in the medieval knightly system, with its religious, moral, and social code. He also learned, at first hand, the methods that would enable him to retain his throne in the years to come. Although succession to the throne was hereditary, wealthy nobles, known as boyars, could elect the heir from among various eligible royal family members. Assassinations and the overthrow of rivals were thus commonplace under this system, and

Vlad II had claimed the Wallachian throne for himself by killing a rival, a method that Vlad III would also adopt.

In 1448, with the support of the Turks, Vlad III came to the throne following the death of his father. He was soon forced to surrender the throne, but regained it by killing the incumbent, Vladislov II. So began Vlad's main period of rule, which lasted from 1456 until 1462.

Just as his father had fought against the Islamic threat, Vlad III saw it as his role to defend the Romanian people against the Ottoman Turks and establish independence and sovereignty. He made Tirgoviste his capital, and set about building his castle in the mountains. So began Vlad's reign of terror, much of which was vested in his desire to eradicate the boyars, and to exact revenge on them for their part in the

OPPOSITE & PAGES 148 & 149: Sighisoara, Transylvania, where Vlad Tepes was born in 1431.

RIGHT: The supposed birthplace of Vlad Tepes in Sighisoara.

deaths of his father and brother. It was also his intention to decimate this powerful class of potentially threatening nobles, and at the same time destroy the age-old system of choosing a successor and replace it with something more to his own liking. At a feast to which the boyars were invited, Vlad had many of them rounded up and murdered on the spot, while others were forced to work on the construction of his castle until the clothes fell from their bodies and they died from exhaustion. But the boyars were not the only focus of his brutal killings; Vlad also threatened his less high-born subjects, establishing a morality of his own whose infringement often resulted in painful, lingering deaths. No one was safe from his attentions, be they women, children, simple peasants, traders, or even foreign ambassadors.

Vlad's favorite method of execution was to impale his victims on stakes, the same method by which he had killed the boyars at the feast. It is said that 100,000 people perished by this method alone, although it was by no means the only way of killing that Vlad enjoyed. Impaling was a slow and excruciatingly painful way to die, and Vlad devised plenty of variations on the theme, from pushing the stake up into the body through the buttocks, to impaling the victim through the chest. Decaying corpses were often left for months, their stakes still in place (much

In această casă a locuit
intre anii 1431–1435,
domnitorul Țării Românești
VLAD DRACUL,
fiul lui
Mircea cel Bătrin

LEFT: A plaque on the wall of the birthplace of Vlad Tepes in Sighisoara.

OPPOSITE LEFT & RIGHT: A statue and a waxwork of Vlad Tepes.

VLAD TEPES

like entomologists display specimens on pins), as a warning to others. In addition to impalings, Vlad also relished other methods of execution and mutilation, such as driving nails through people's heads, cutting off ears and noses, skinning victims alive, or throwing them to wild animals.

Eventually, however, the ever-present and powerful Turks were able to force Vlad to abandon his castle for gloomy, mist-shrouded Transylvania. There he asked for assistance from Matthius Corvinus, the king of Hungary, but instead of cooperating, the king had

OPPOSITE & LEFT: Poenari Castle, a stronghold of Vlad Tepes in Romania.

ABOVE: Matthius Corvinus, king of Hungary from 1458.

VLAD TEPES

Vlad arrested and confined in a tower. After four years as Matthius's prisoner in Buda, he was again reinstated as ruler of Wallachia. In 1474, determined to win back his throne, he was given command of a contingent of soldiers with which he re-entered the principality.

During fights against the Turks, thousands of Ottoman prisoners were impaled and left to die on the banks of the Danube outside Vlad's capital of Tirgoviste.

Vlad died in mysterious circumstances in 1475, and his body was

1871 *Carmilla*, in which a lonely young woman is preyed upon by a female vampire. The image of a vampire as an aristocrat, moreover, had already been created by John Polidori in "The Vampyre" (1819), written after the summer of 1816 was spent with Mary Shelley (the creator of *Frankenstein)*, her husband, the poet Percy Bysshe Shelley, and Lord Byron. The famous Lyceum Theatre in London, where Stoker worked between 1878 and 1898, had as its actor-manager Henry Irving, who was Stoker's real-life inspiration for the central character, and who excelled in gentlemanly though villainous roles.

Until a few weeks before publication in May 1897, Stoker's manuscript had been entitled, *The Un-Dead*, and the name of the subject of the story was "Count Wampyr." In the meantime, however, Stoker had become somewhat intrigued by the name "Dracula," after reading

buried in the church of the Snagov Monastery. In 1935, a richly dressed but beheaded corpse was exhumed at Snagov, the head, supposedly, having been sent as a gift to the Turkish sultan.

Dracula and the Vlad Connection
Bram Stoker's vampire novel may be the most famous of its type but it was not the first, and may have received some inspiration from Sheridan Le Fanu's

ABOVE LEFT: Snagov Monastery, where Vlad Tepes is said to have been buried.

OPPOSITE: Dracula/Vlad Tepes souvenirs on sale in Sighisoara.

or drink their blood, believing that it preserved her youth, which may explain why Dracula is said to appear younger after feeding on blood.

Stoker is thought to have received historical information on the subject from Ármin Vámbéry, a Hungarian professor he met at least twice. But there is neither record of correspondence between the two, nor is Vámbéry mentioned in Stoker's notes for *Dracula*.

William Wilkinson's book, *An Account of the Principalities of Wallachia and Moldavia*

ABOVE: *A scene from Sheridan Le Fanu's novel Carmilla.*

RIGHT: *Countess Elizabeth Báthory.*

OPPOSITE, PAGES 160 & 161: *Bran Castle, which Vlad Tepes used during his incursions into Transylvania.*

with Political Observations Relative to Them (London 1820), which he had discovered in the Whitby Library, and around which Yorkshire seaside town some of the action of his own novel was set.

It has also been suggested that Stoker was influenced by the history of Countess Elizabeth Báthory, born in the kingdom of Hungary in 1560. Báthory is suspected of having tortured and killed many young women in order to bathe in

CHAPTER NINE
LAND OF THE VAMPIRE

Transylvania, the region to which Vlad III fled before launching his bid to retake the throne of Wallachia, and the main setting for Bram Stoker's Gothic tale, today occupies a large portion of north-western Romania. It is a place with a tumultuous history, where many cultures, including Romanian, Hungarian, and Rroma, have converged.

It was the nucleus of the Roman province of Dacia in around 106 CE, the name Romania indicating its Roman connections, and it later featured in the empires of the Visigoths, the Huns, the Magyars, and others. Medieval sites from this rich historical past abound, and castles and fortified churches add to the feeling of time having stood still.

RIGHT & OPPOSITE: Transylvania is encircled to the south and east by the brooding Carpathian Mountains. It is a haunted place, hiding many dark secrets.

OPPOSITE: Today, Transylvania is a historical region in the center of Romania.

ABOVE, PAGES 166 & 167: The highest peaks of the Carpathian Mountains are known as the Transylvanian Alps.

Transylvania is encircled to the south and east by the tall, brooding peaks of the Carpathian Mountains; indeed, the highest crags are in the part known as the Transylvanian Alps. Even today, it seems a fertile land in which dark myths and legends can be seen to flourish, and a place where the secrets of the past are only slowly and reluctantly given up. No wonder, then, that the writer Emily Gerard (best-known for the influence her collections of

LAND OF THE VAMPIRE

Transylvanian folklore had on Bram Stoker's *Dracula*) was moved to comment, in her 1888 book, *The Land Beyond the Forest,* that it would appear that "… the whole species of demons, pixies, witches, and hobgoblins … had taken refuge within this mountain rampart …."

Emily Gerard, whose husband was a Hungarian officer, and who herself lived in Transylvania for two years, went on to describe other mysterious and mythical aspects of the region in similarly colorful

Visitors to Transylvania get the distinct feeling that they are in a land where time has stood still.

terms. She noted, for example, that the place was riddled with numerous caverns that might harbor evil spirits; it had forest glades suited only to fairy folk; there was golden treasure hidden in deep mountain gorges; and there were isolated lakes that seemed to call up visions of water sprites. In all, she felt

that the whole ambience of the place did much to plant in the imaginative minds of the Romanians, the area's oldest inhabitants, a "code of fanciful superstition," to which they clung as tightly as they did to their religion.

She goes on to suggest that other forces were at work here, too, including the ancient customs and beliefs imported many hundreds of years ago by Saxon colonists, for example, and maintained here even more fervently than in their original homeland. Then there were the superstitious beliefs of the numerous roaming gypsy tribes, that traversed the countryside in their caravans, spreading their dark tales as they went. Evocative names, such as Gania Drakuluj, "Devil's Mountain," abound in Transylvania, and served merely to highlight the feeling strong within the population that they were indeed a people surrounded by dark and powerful influences.

This is an ancient place, with a long and varied history that seems to have left its mark upon the landscape, encouraging superstitious beliefs and strange customs.

LAND OF THE VAMPIRE

The first Rroma that arrived in Europe wandered from country to country, recounting, as they went, extraordinary and mysterious stories concerning their origins.

Flames and Treasures

According to Emily Gerard, the most important day of the year was St. George's Day (April 23), the eve of which was marked by all manner of witches' sabbaths in lonely caverns or within the confines of the walls of ruins. To ward off the influence of witches, and to prevent them from gaining entry to houses or stables, great blocks of turf were placed over the windows and front doors of every building and, as an extra

precaution, the peasants would frequently keep watch all through the night by their sleeping cattle. This same night was believed to be the best time for finding treasure, and many could be found roaming the hills searching for gold in the earth. Futile and superstitious though such searches may have seemed, there were elements of pragmatism in such fervent activity, for nowhere else was there a nation where generation upon generation had found it necessary to secrete their valuables and beat hasty retreats in the face of advancing armies. But genuine seams of silver and gold did indeed run through the earth in all directions, making a chance discovery a real, albeit remote, possibility.

During the night of St. George's Day, according to legend, all the treasures within the earth begin to burn with a bluish flame, and in doing so guide the lucky few to the places where they are concealed. Such lights, seen before midnight, indicate the

The eve of St. George's Day was a time when witches held their sabbaths in old ruins or lonely caverns.

whereabouts of treasure kept safe by kindly spirits, but lights that appear after that hour are to be avoided at all costs. There must then follow a strict ritual if the treasure is to be recovered, which involves plunging a knife through the rags that cover the right foot (Romanian peasants used to wrap their feet in rags before encasing them in rough leather sandals), and then hurling the knife towards the flame. Once treasure is removed, the person finding it must ensure that nothing is used to fill the hole from which the treasure has been taken, or a rapid death will ensue.

Other Monsters of Transylvania

At the time when Emily Gerard was making her observations regarding the cult of the vampire in Transylvania, and of fiends in general, she makes the point that there was a belief in the existence of

LEFT: During the night of St. George's Day, the earth emits blue flames to guide treasure-hunters.

OPPOSITE: Not only were there vampires, but werewolves also roamed abroad.

two distinct types of vampires, living as well as dead, with living vampires usually being the offspring of unmarried parents, although those born within wedlock were not necessarily immune. The old remedies for dealing with vampires – such as driving stakes through their hearts, cutting off their heads, and so on – were still used on occasions. And as if vampires themselves weren't trouble enough, other hellish creatures, including werewolves, also flourished in the land.

There is a chilling story concerning a man and his wife when they were returning home from church one Sunday. The man, who unbeknown to his wife was, in fact, a werewolf, suddenly felt himself about to take the form of the dire creature. So he rushed into some nearby bushes to allow the transformation to take place. Soon afterwards, his wife, who had been waiting nearby, was suddenly set upon by what she took to be a ferocious dog, which bit her badly and tore her dress. The alarmed woman fled for home alone, only to be greeted by her smiling husband. As he smiled, the wife was

various types of supernatural beings, including the Miase Nopte, a night spirit whose activities make it dangerous to leave the house after dark, and the Dschuma, an evil-doer that causes illness or plague to befall a village, and which can only be defended against by hanging, at the entrance to the village, a red shirt that must be made in a certain way by seven women, all working together on the project during one night. Most feared of all these spirits, however, is the *strigoi*, based on the ancient Greek *strix,* a vampiric entity

LEFT & BELOW: Stories and images of werewolves are as prevalent as those of vampires in Transylvania.

OPPOSITE: The strigoi, based on the Greek strix, that gave its name to a genus of owl, is a vampiric spirit that is greatly feared.

that can come into being when funeral rites are incorrectly performed. The ghoulish character of the *strigoi* is unusual: first, it may take the form almost of an invisible poltergeist, bedevilling people by moving furniture around or stealing articles, such as food.

horrified to glimpse some shreds of her dress caught between his teeth. There are many such tales of encounters with werewolves, which is perhaps not surprising in a remote and mountainous land in which real-life wolves were abundant and where superstitious folk might have mistaken the animals' natural cunning for something altogether more supernatural.

Even today, there are many people ready to attest to the existence of

Then it becomes visible, assuming the form of the deceased person when they were alive, but continuing to steal, beg for food, and even causing disease. In the end, the *strigoi* turns its attention to feeding on human beings, beginning with members of the deceased's family, and may even suck blood directly from its victim's heart.

By considering only a few of the many myths and legends of the region, we begin to see how a tale like that of Dracula would have found credence in the remote mountains and valleys of this remote region, with its population of spirit- and demon-fearing peasant folk. Transylvania is by no means the only place where vampires were feared, but it is perhaps the one, above all others, where one can imagine such dark forces bringing terror to an isolated, possibly already susceptible, population.

Bran Castle

In southern Transylvania, on its border with Wallachia and near to the city of Brasov, lies the impressive Gothic and Renaissance fortress known as Bran Castle. It was originally a wooden

construction, erected in 1212 by the Teutonic Knights, but which was destroyed by Mongols in 1242. In 1377 the Saxon inhabitants of Brasov rebuilt the castle in stone, at their own expense. Thereafter it was used variously in defense against the Ottoman Empire, as a customs post on the mountain pass between Transylvania and Wallachia, and as a royal residence. Today, the castle is a museum open to tourists.

Rising from a rocky height and flanked by dense woodland, the castle dominates all it surveys, providing panoramic views of the high, lonely mountains beyond. Even the village of Bran, sprawling beneath the ramparts, is one where one might imagine its inhabitants being stricken with awe, and even fear of, the sinister structure looming far above. But for many, Bran Castle's real fascination lies in the tantalizing thought that not only might it

OPPOSITE & RIGHT: It would seem that Vlad Tepes's association with Bran Castle may be tenuous. There is no evidence that he lived there, but he may have been held prisoner there for a while.

Bran Castle would seem to be the perfect home of the aristocratic Count Dracula, of Bram Stoker's tale, and even though there is no truth in the story, the castle makes the most of its tenuous links with Vlad Tepes and the Dracula myth.

have been the refuge of Vlad Tepes, but also that of Dracula, Bram Stoker's aristocratic vampire.

Sadly, it seems, such hopes are destined to be dashed on both counts, though the Romanian authorities may dearly wish that it could be otherwise, for it would make the castle an even greater magnet for tourists. First, there is no historical evidence that Bran Castle was the stronghold of the notorious and sadistic Vlad Tepes, although it is believed he may have spent a few days incarcerated there when the Ottoman Empire controlled Transylvania. Second, the castle in Bram Stoker's novel is set some distance away from Bran, on the Borgo Pass near Bistritz in north-central Transylvania.

But Vlad Tepes did indeed have a great castle of his own in the region; after all, there are accounts of boyars

and others perishing in their droves
while laboring to rebuild it. Where, then,
is the authentic castle of Dracula? For
the answer to that question, thanks must
be given to two researchers – Radu
Florescu and Raymond McNally – who
set out with the intention of answering
this question. Their searches, however,
took them much farther south, to a place
in the Wallachian Mountains above the
Arges river valley. Here, perched on a
craggy outcrop, they came upon the
ruined battlements of Poenari Castle,
discovering that they were only a part of
a greater complex known as the Royal
Court of Tirgoviste.

   To reach this place requires a long
and dangerous uphill trek of 1,500 steps,
making it the kind of inaccessible lair
that Vlad Tepes would have favored
most. During Vlad's reign, the castle
survived bombardment by gunfire from
the invading Turks, only to fall into ruins
as the result of earthquakes later on.
Today, the gaunt castle walls, as well as
the restored Chindia Tower and the part
of the complex known as the Princely
Court, can be seen clearly outlined
against the sky. Although Poenari is now

a tourist attraction and yet another part of the lucrative Dracula tourist trail, the ghostly echoes of the cries of the long-since dead, the victims of Vlad's reign of terror, can almost be heard after all these years. No wonder it is thought to be one of the most haunted places in the world.

The Curse of Tirgoviste

But the name of Tirgoviste, while it is synonymous with the bloody excesses of Vlad Tepes, has yet another link with a gruesome past. In 1965 the politician Nicolae Ceausescu became secretary-general of the Romanian Communist

BELOW: Poenari Castle may be seen from the incredible Transfagarasan Road that winds through the Carpathian Mountains.

OPPOSITE: Nicolae Ceausescu.

Party. In 1967 he was promoted president of the Council of State, then

in 1974 became president of Romania. The beginning of Ceausescu's time as president began well enough. Within the country he gained popularity by maintaining the stance taken by his predecessor, Gheorghe Gheorghiu-Dej, who had succeeded in getting Soviet troops withdrawn from Romania, and he adopted an independent policy towards its giant Soviet neighbor to the east. As far as the West was concerned, he was also regarded as someone with whom it "could do business," for he had adopted an open policy towards Western Europe and the United States of America, in sharp contrast to that taken by most other Warsaw Pact members at the time, which viewed the West with extreme suspicion to say the least. Under Ceausescu, Romania became the first communist country to welcome an American president when Richard Nixon visited the country. Official visits by Ceausescu to other Western countries followed, and Ceausescu even began to assume the role of mediator in international affairs.

But Ceausescu's rule was to become increasingly erratic, blemished by a deterioration in foreign relations with the West as well as with the Soviet Union. Within the country he was not only refusing to implement the kind of liberal reforms that were beginning to take place elsewhere, but was also introducing

a socialist program of systemization, resulting in demolition, resettlement, and construction in the countryside. Over one-fifth of central Bucharest was destroyed, including many fine churches and historical buildings, so that Ceausescu could rebuild the city according to his own whims. He also planned to bulldoze many of the villages, moving their inhabitants into city apartment blocks as part of his programs of industrialization and urbanization.

Other unpopular measures included banning abortion in 1966, and heavily taxing people who were still childless after the age of 25. Through ignorance and perversity, the incidence of HIV/AIDS grew alarmingly in the country, and homelessness, child abandonment, and other social problems began to increase, while political indoctrination and the suppression of freedom of expression became part of a neo-Stalinist offensive imposed by the regime. Financial incompetence meant that foreign debts soared, contributing to the devastation of the economy. Soon there were serious shortages of food and

everyday essential items, bringing extreme hardship to everyone concerned. Meanwhile, Ceausescu seemed to be in complete denial of the steadily worsening domestic situation and decline in living standards, and propaganda films were released showing the country's leader inside stores stocked with all the essential goods the people knew were unavailable to them.

Eventually, the unrest reached unprecedented levels, and a mass meeting in Bucharest on December 21, 1989, in what is now known as Revolution Square, was the beginning of a countrywide rebellion. During the upheavals that followed, security forces loyal to Ceausescu are thought to have killed about 1,000 people, although reports current at the time put the figure at nearly 64,000. Ceausescu and his wife, Elena, fled by helicopter to Tirgoviste but were apprehended by police before being turned over to the army. A short trial ensued on Christmas Day 1989, during which Ceausescu was accused of crimes that included genocide. He and his wife were found guilty and sentenced to death, their execution ensuing almost

BELOW: Ceausescu and his wife fled Bucharest by helicopter to Tirgoviste, where they were captured and eventually executed.

OPPOSITE: Ceausescu's palace in Bucharest, now the Palace of the Parliament.

immediately by firing squad. Thus ended the life of Nicolae Ceausescu, a modern-day tyrant with similarities to Vlad Tepes. Perhaps his biggest crime was his refusal to understand and implement the liberal measures already being adopted by the Soviet bloc under Mikhail Gorbachev.

CHAPTER TEN
DRACULA, LORD OF VAMPIRES

Of all the tales of vampires that have passed from generation to generation, the legend of the one known as Dracula strikes the deepest chord, his being the supreme embodiment of depravity and evil recounted so chillingly in Bram Stoker's famous novel, and without whose inclusion no account of vampires would be complete. Yet herein lies a great paradox, for of all the accounts of vampires given here and elsewhere – many of them recounted by living people, including some purporting to have witnessed the phenomenon itself – the most famous of them all comes directly from a work of fiction. So

RIGHT: A modern representation of Count Dracula, the archetypal vampire.

OPPOSITE: An ancient map of Transylvania, showing Bistritz, the home of Dracula, near to its central eastern limits.

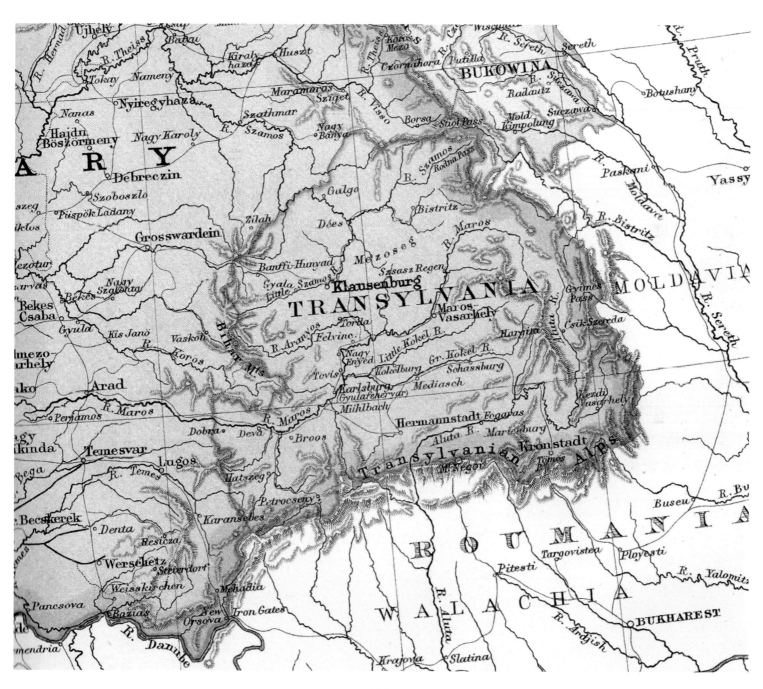

LEFT: The ancient town of Sighisoara is the birthplace of Vlad Tepes, whose story inspired Bram Stoker to write *Dracula*.

ABOVE: Bram Stoker, who researched the vampire myths of Transylvania before writing his seminal novel.

OPPOSITE LEFT: Vlad Tepes or Vlad Dracul – the prototype of Stoker's Dracula?

OPPOSITE RIGHT: Count Dracula lives in a castle in the shadow of the Carpathian Mountains, near the Borgo Pass.

graphic and so vivid is this tale of morbid Gothic horror, that our by-now overstimulated imaginations are almost unable to resist the belief that here is a true and awful episode from beyond the realms of normality. So complete is this transportation, that Dracula, himself the archetypal vampire, has created a genre that shows no signs of diminishment.

Who Was Dracula?

Unlike so many of the vampires of eastern European legend and elsewhere, Dracula is no simple peasant from a remote and impoverished village,

BELOW: *Dracula's handsome exterior belies the evil within.*

FAR RIGHT: *Bran Castle epitomizes everything Bram Stoker had in mind when he describes Dracula's brooding castle.*

returned from the dead to trouble his kinsfolk and neighbors. Instead, we know him as Count Dracula, a high-born Transylvanian nobleman of Hungarian extraction, who claims to be able to trace his lineage all the way back to Attila the

fiery red. His anger is apparent, for example, when Dracula attacks the three female vampires that inhabit his castle for their insubordination in attempting to seduce and devour Jonathan Harker (an unwilling guest). Dracula is fiercely proud of his warrior lineage and also seems to have an admiration for the British Empire, no doubt being more than interested in the nature of extreme power.

LEFT: A cartoon rendering of Count Dracula.

BELOW & OPPOSITE: Dracula has the ability to shape-shift as a bat or even a wolf.

Within the novel, Dracula is credited with various supernatural powers: according to another of his would-be adversaries, Abraham Van Helsing,

Hun. Count Dracula dwells in a brooding castle in the Carpathian Mountains near the Borgo Pass in north-central Transylvania. As befits a man of such high breeding, Dracula exudes an easy air of aristocratic charm, belying the true evil lying within. Early in life, Dracula is said to have been a student of the black arts, his mastery of them enabling him to attain an immortality of sorts as a vampire.

In Bram Stoker's novel, Dracula, on the surface, is gentlemanly and cordial, but he is subject to terrifying fits of rage when thwarted, when his eyes turn to a

Dracula is blessed with the physical strength of 20 men and can perform gravity-defying feats, such as climbing down vertical walls like a lizard. Like other powerful vampires, Dracula uses mind-controlling techniques, such as hypnotism, to subdue his victims, and he is also able to call upon creatures of the night to do his bidding when required. Dracula is able to shape-shift at will, variously becoming a rat, a bat, a wolf, or even inanimate objects such as fog or vapor. This shape-shifting ability is possible at dawn, noon, dusk, and at night. He can muster up mists in which to conceal himself, and can even call up storms at sea.

Dracula's powers are diminished significantly during the hours of daylight, and he is repulsed by the presence of garlic and crucifixes. He can only cross running water at low or high tides, and can only enter a place if he is first invited to do so; but once this invitation has been offered, he can enter and leave at

Dracula can conjure up mists in which to conceal himself and can even call up storms at sea.

196

will. In true vampire style, Dracula needs only fresh blood to sustain and rejuvenate him, and in the process of regaining his strength as he sleeps, needs access to Transylvanian soil.

An interesting aspect of Stoker's novel is the notion of vampirism as a contagious disease, in which the vampire passes on its own demonic affliction to its victim in turn.

The Story of Dracula

Stoker's tale of Dracula is recounted by the adversaries of the vampire themselves, mainly in the form of letters and entries in journals. The story begins in the late 19th century, with Dracula poised to embark on his long-held plan for world domination. Jonathan Harker, a junior English solicitor, travels from England, by means of boat, train, and carriage, to arrive at Count Dracula's decaying castle, set in the remote Carpathian Mountains near the border between Transylvania and Moldova. The purpose of Harker's visit is to provide

OPPOSITE & RIGHT: Dracula is repulsed by crucifixes and garlic.

Dracula with legal advice, in order to facilitate a property transaction that is being overseen by Peter Hawkins, Harker's employer in Exeter, England. Harker's progress towards Castle Dracula fills him with more than a few misgivings, especially when he is warned by locals of the perils that lie in wait. There is worse to follow: the count has sent his own carriage and driver to take his guest on the last part of the journey; at one stage, the carriage halts and the driver disembarks, only to suddenly go missing. Then wolves surround the carriage, causing the horses to become extremely agitated. Gripped with fear, Harker is relieved to see the driver reappear, but becomes more than alarmed by his ability to control the wolves.

Arriving at the castle, Harker comes face to face with his host for the first

OPPOSITE: In Stoker's novel, the notion that vampires pass on their affliction, like a contagious disease, is explored.

RIGHT: A page of Bram Stoker's notes for Dracula.

time. Count Dracula is a tall, thin, aged man with a white moustache. He is dressed all in black. To begin with, Harker is reassured by the count's seemingly hospitable welcome and fine manners, but he is informed that Dracula will not always be able to join Harker for meals. Over dinner that night, Harker notices the count's unusually sharp teeth and extremely ruddy lips. They begin to discuss the purchase of a large, empty property in Purfleet called Carfax.

The next day, the count enters his room while Harker is shaving. Harker notices that the count casts no reflection in the mirror, and finding this unnerving, accidentally cuts himself, whereupon the count makes a lunge at Harker's throat, only to be repulsed when he touches the beads holding a crucifix around Harker's neck. Dracula breaks the mirror and leaves Harker, muttering: "…it is more dangerous than you think in this country."

Harker is driven in Dracula's own carriage for the last part of the journey to the castle. On the way, he is alarmed when the carriage is encircled by wolves, and even more so at the driver's seeming ability to control them.

Harker's extreme disquiet is further increased when he discovers that, far from being a welcome guest, he is in fact a prisoner in the gloomy castle. One night he is seduced, then almost killed, by the Brides of Dracula, three voracious female vampires, only to be rescued at the last minute by Dracula himself. It is Dracula's intention, however, to keep Harker alive long enough to obtain the legal advice he needs and to learn more about England and London, which is his planned destination. By now fearing for his life, Harker tries several times to leave the castle, first by bribing gypsies to post letters, telling his employer and fiancée of his plight, but his scheme is foiled. Then he demands the count allow him to return to England, but as the door to the castle is opened he is confronted by hungry wolves, making escape impossible. But Harker has another plan: earlier, he had seen the count scaling the vertical walls of the castle (another worrying sight at the time), and he now makes his escape by climbing out of a window.

Back in England, we meet Mina Murray, Harker's fiancée, who is becoming worried, having had no news of Harker for some time. We also meet, among others, her friend Lucy Westenra, as well as Dr. Seward, who is in charge of a lunatic asylum. One of Seward's patients, Renfield, has the peculiar habit of catching and eating animals, such as spiders, flies, and other insects, in the belief that they will make him strong through his absorption of their life force.

Mina visits Lucy at the seaside town of Whitby, in Yorkshire, in the north of England. While she is there, a Russian ship, the *Demeter*, is wrecked on the shore nearby during a fierce storm. Mysteriously, all members of the ship's crew are found to be missing, apart from the dead captain. The only sign of life aboard the stricken vessel is a large wolflike dog that is seen to leap ashore, then quickly disappear into the

Harker is almost killed by the Brides of Dracula, but is rescued by Dracula himself at the very last minute.

In the novel, Lucy Westenra is seen sleepwalking in the graveyard of St. Mary's Church, Whitby.

surrounding countryside. The only cargo found on board are some boxes of soil shipped from Castle Dracula. The ship's log, however, tells of mysterious events that have taken place on the fateful sea journey.

Soon afterwards, Lucy begins to sleepwalk, and Mina finds Lucy, one night, in the cemetery in the town, with what she believes to be a dark shape with glowing red eyes bending over her. Lucy gradually becomes weaker and more sick; she also bears red marks on her throat. Lucy cannot account for these marks, and neither can Dr. Seward, who asks his old mentor, Professor Van Helsing, to help him arrive at a satisfactory diagnosis.

Meanwhile, Harker surfaces in Budapest, suffering from "brain fever," and Mina goes to join him there. Van Helsing arrives in Whitby to examine Lucy, then orders that her room be hung with garlic — a traditional method of warding off vampires. At first, the

LEFT: The famous 199 steps leading from the harbor up to Whitby Abbey.

OPPOSITE: The abbey's imposing ruins.

cure seems to work, for Lucy begins to recover. But her mother, unaware of the purpose of the garlic, removes it from Lucy's room, leaving her daughter vulnerable to attack once more. Despite giving Lucy blood transfusions, in an attempt to revive her, the efforts of her doctors are in vain, for one night a wolf enters the house, frightening Lucy's mother to death before killing Lucy.

Van Helsing is convinced that, by now, Lucy has entered the realms of the undead – in other words, that she is now a vampire. His suspicions are confirmed when she is discovered attacking a child. All agree she must be destroyed, and they decide to perform a ritual that will enable her soul to rest in peace. While the undead Lucy sleeps, her former suitor, Arthur Holmwood, plunges a stake through her heart. Then her head is cut off and her mouth filled with garlic.

They now all vow to destroy Dracula himself, a task in which the group are

joined by the now-recuperated Harker, together with Mina, who have since married. They attempt to piece together the various journal entries that Harker, Seward, and others have written, in the hope that they will be led to Dracula. One night, however, Dracula finds and attacks Mina, also feeding her with some of his own blood to create a spiritual bond in order to control her. Mina slowly succumbs, alternatively drifting from a state of consciousness into one of semi-trance during which she is telepathically connected with Dracula.

It is this connection that the group begins to use, and Mina is hypnotized by Van Helsing to discover Dracula's movements. The connection gradually weakens as they make their way to Dracula's castle, which they cleanse by killing the three female vampires and blocking the castle entrances with sacred objects. Dracula reaches his castle at sundown, where he is caught and killed with knives, driven through his throat and heart, but not before Dracula's gypsy bodyguards have been destroyed. Dracula crumbles to dust, and at the same time the curse on Mina is lifted.

Because Dracula was not dispatched in the traditional way, there have since been speculations as to whether or not he was actually destroyed. Could it be that he will rise again at some point in the future?

Ghostly Whitby

While Transylvania will always be the ultimate setting for the tale of Dracula, Whitby, quite rightly, has a large part to play, having unbreakable links with the story. It is fitting, perhaps, that Bram Stoker should have chosen this north-eastern English port as the setting for several chapters. The town lies on a rugged sweep of windy coastline, a likely place for a ship like the *Demeter* to have run aground in foul weather. Whitby is an old-established community with a long history of supernatural goings-on, beginning well before the time of Dracula. Adding significantly to its general eeriness are the huge, gaunt, arched ruins of Whitby Abbey, which has connections with St. Hilda as well as with Captain James Cook, the great explorer, and which loom over the red

The cliffs and North Sea around Whitby.

pantile-roofed houses that crowd the quayside below.

Not surprisingly, Whitby has become yet another part of the Dracula tourist industry that has grown up to exploit the enduring interest in this most famous of vampires. A highlight for any fan is the Bram Stoker Memorial Seat, from which spot Stoker was inspired to add the Whitby scenes in his novel, and from where both the ruins of the abbey and the dangerous, rocky coastline are clearly visible. An inscription on the seat reads: "The view from this spot inspired Bram Stoker (1847–1912) to use Whitby as the setting of part of his world-famous novel DRACULA. This seat was erected by Scarborough Borough Council and the Dracula Society to mark the 68th Anniversary of Stoker's death: April 20th 1980." Interest in Dracula within the town is such that there is also a Whitby Dracula Society, dedicated to commemorating the events in the novel.

But what of Whitby's other links with the supernatural? Sightings of ghosts are numerous, and indeed the town is reputedly one of the most haunted places in Britain. The ghostly form of St. Hilda,

the founder of Whitby Abbey, who died in 680 CE, has allegedly been seen in one of the windows.

Interestingly, the old Benedictine abbey does not actually figure in Stoker's *Dracula*, except in passing. Instead, it is St. Mary's Church that features strongly in the novel. This fortresslike, hilltop church is also a dominating and ominous structure, with commanding views over the harbor and beyond out to sea. Within the grounds of this same church, Mina espies her doomed friend, Lucy Westenra, while she is sleepwalking one night, with Dracula himself, of course, in the act of draining the lifeblood from her body.

That Dracula should have performed his dread deeds on hallowed ground confirms even more forcibly the special evil that he represents. Stoker not only addresses the battle between good and evil: the keen reader will also notice that all manner of social and political issues are uncovered as the novel progresses.

The red pantile-roofed houses that crowd the harbor of Whitby.

CHAPTER ELEVEN

THE VAMPIRE IN BOOK & FILM

While Count Dracula, of course, tops the vampire genre, it is fair to say that other lesser-known examples also feature widely in popular fiction. Vampires appear in art, in poetry, in novels, and as characters in films, television shows, and plays. There are even comical vampires, as well as vampires created as children's toys. The vampire, elusive though it may be in corporeal form, is alive and well, and is indeed thriving and expanding in popular culture. What follows is a brief look at some of the most important examples of the genre, remembering, of course, that there is much more for the fan to enjoy than there is space to mention here.

Vampires in Literature

The vampire, as a subject for popular fiction, has its origins in the 18th century, starting with poetry. These include the short German poem *Der Vampir*, written in 1748 by Heinrich August Ossenfelder. There are strong erotic overtones here, in which a man, rejected by a pious maiden, threatens to visit her at night to drink her blood. There are also examples of tales describing how the dead might return to their loved ones, bringing death to them in their turn.

Gottfried August Bürger explored this theme in the 1773 poem *Lenore* and from which Bram Stoker quotes a snippet – "For the dead travel fast" – in his novel *Dracula*. In the 1797 poem *The Bride of Corinth,* by Johann Wolfgang von Goethe (the influential German writer, polymath and creator of *Faust*, the man who promises his soul to the devil in return for knowledge), a young woman returns from the grave to search for her betrothed. The girl, from a Christian background, is forced by her mother to break off the engagement with her

DER VAMPIR
My dear young maiden clingeth
Unbending, fast and firm
To all the long-held teaching
Of a mother ever true;
As in vampires unmortal
Folk on the Theyse's portal
Heyduck-like do believe.
But my Christine thou dost dally,
And wilt my loving parry
Till I myself avenging
To a vampire's health a-drinking
Him toast in pale tockay.

And as softly thou art sleeping
To thee shall I come creeping
And thy life's blood drain away.
And so shalt thou be trembling
For thus shall I be kissing
And death's threshold thou' it be crossing
With fear, in my cold arms.
And last shall I thee question
Compared to such instruction
What are a mother's charms?

Heinrich August Ossenfelder, 1748

pagan lover. She becomes a nun, but is eventually driven to her death before appearing again as a revenant. Here we see an example of the conflict between paganism and Christianity that often features in vampirism.

In English literature, the vampire is first mentioned in the 1797 epic 12 "book" poem of Robert Southey, entitled *Thalaba the Destroyer*, in which Thalaba's deceased love, Oneiza, has become a vampire. Written around the same time, but not published until 1816, Samuel Taylor Coleridge's poem *Christabel* was another influence, with Christabel being seduced by a supernatural female entity by the name of Geraldine. This is similar to the theme of *Carmilla*, a Gothic novella by Joseph Sheridan Le Fanu. This was published in 1872, and tells the tale of a young woman, Laura, who becomes the victim of the female vampire Carmilla, the story becoming the model for the spate of female and lesbian vampirism that followed. Carmilla has much in common with the vampire

An etching illustrating Christabel, *by Samuel Taylor Coleridge.*

legends; she causes her victims to experience nightmares of being bitten by a fiendish figure; she causes her victims to become progressively sicker because of her attentions; she sleeps in a coffin; she can shape-shift at will, frequently assuming the form of a huge black cat; and in the end she is destroyed after first being exhumed from her hidden tomb.

In 1813 the English poet, Lord Byron, wrote *The Giaour*, an epic poem with allusions to the traditional vampire of folklore. A few years later, Byron's own wild and raffish lifestyle became the inspiration for one of the most important stories of the time, "The Vampyre," published in 1819 by John William Polidori and featuring the fictional vampire Lord Ruthven (*see* page 39 et seq.).

The 19th century also saw several stage performances on the theme. Charles Nodier adapted Polidori's story into a stage melodrama, *Le Vampire*, also producing an unauthorized sequel to

Joseph Sheridan Le Fanu's Carmilla is the story of an innocent girl, Laura, who becomes a victim of Carmilla, a female vampire.

Polidori's original story. Nodier's play was then adapted by an English dramatist, James Planché, as *The Vampire or The Bride of the Isles* in 1820. Nodier's play was also the inspiration for an opera entitled, *Der Vampyr*, by the German composer Heinrich Marschner. Unlike Nodier's play, which was set in Scotland, the location of this work was the more likely and traditional setting of Wallachia, a region of Romania to the south of the Carpathian Mountains. A character called Sir Alan Raby appears in another play of the time, *The Vampire* (1852), written by the Irish actor and playwright Dion Boucicault, who took the lead role himself, to mixed reviews. The English monarch, Queen Victoria, was present at a performance and was not amused, describing the play as "very trashy."

The year 1828 saw the publication of another vampire tale, *The Skeleton Count or The Vampire Mistress*. This was unusual in that it is believed to have been the first such story written by a woman. The author was Elizabeth Caroline Grey, a prolific and wide-ranging English Victorian writer who produced over 30 romantic novels,

Gothic tales, and other sensational fiction. Among the publications to which she contributed were the penny dreadfuls which, as the name implies, could be bought for a penny and contained stories that were lurid, gruesome, and sensational in their subject matter. Printed on cheap pulp paper and aimed mainly at working-class adolescents, the stories were usually published in serial form over several weeks.

Many of the tales had Gothic overtones, and it wasn't long before vampires began to feature within the pages, including the tale of *Varney the Vampire or The Feast of Blood* (*see* page 28). This Gothic horror, by James Malcolm Rymer, appeared between 1845 and 1847 and was a tale of considerable length, running to over 850 double-column pages. The story is set in the early 18th century, and deals with the problems that the vampire, Sir Francis Varney, inflicts upon the Bannerworths, a wealthy family brought to the point of financial ruin by their lately deceased father.

Varney himself is said to have been cursed with vampirism after betraying a Royalist to the English republican general

Oliver Cromwell, and then accidentally killing his own son. Like many later fictional vampires, Varney has fangs that leave tell-tale puncture wounds on the necks of his victims. He also has hypnotic powers, superhuman strength, and is given to entering windows at night to attack his victims. But here we see a divergence from what is usually expected of vampires, for Varney has no qualms about appearing in daylight, neither does he have an aversion to those vital weapons in the fight: garlic and holy crosses. Again, unlike later vampires that can sustain themselves only by drinking blood, Varney is able to eat and drink human food, even though it is not his preferred choice.

The story of Varney is interesting in that it appears to portray the vampire as a figure to be pitied: he himself loathes the condition, but he carries on with it in spite of himself. In the end he is driven to suicide by hurling himself into Naples's volcanic Mount Vesuvius.

The story of *Varney the Vampire* had a significant influence on the vampire fiction that followed, and on Bram Stoker's *Dracula*, in particular.

Other European writers also exploited the genre, one such being the French novelist and dramatist Paul Henri Corentin Féval. In addition to writing popular swashbuckling and crime-fighting novels, such as *Le Loup Blanc* in 1843, he followed them with three famous vampire novels: *Le Chevalier Ténèbre* (1860), *La Vampire* (1865), and *La Ville Vampire* (1874). Féval's tales incorporate some familiar and recurring themes. In *La Vampire*, for example, we meet Countess Addhema, a female vampire with a powerful libido, while in *La Ville Vampire* the inspiration may be present for vampire franchises to follow, such as *Buffy the Vampire Slayer*. In *La Ville Vampire*, the vampire protagonist

RIGHT: *La Ville Vampire may have been the inspiration for Buffy the Vampire Slayer (see page 237).*

OPPOSITE LEFT: *Gustave Henri Joseph Le Rouge, author of Le Prisonnier de la Planète Mars.*

OPPOSITE RIGHT: *I Am Legend, a movie based on Richard Matheson's seminal 1954 novel of the same name.*

CAST OF Buffy The Vampire Slayer

was a true-life English writer of Gothic novels by the name of Ann Radcliffe, in which she saves her friends from the feared vampire, Lord Otto Goetzi, by mounting an expedition to discover the legendary vampire city of Selene. In her book of 1879, *Le Capitaine Vampire*, the Belgian writer Marie Nizet features Boris Liatoukine, who besides being a Russian officer is also a vampire.

It would be surprising indeed if the lands that inspired so many of the original European vampire myths did not themselves give rise to novels based on

POSTER ART for I Am Legend

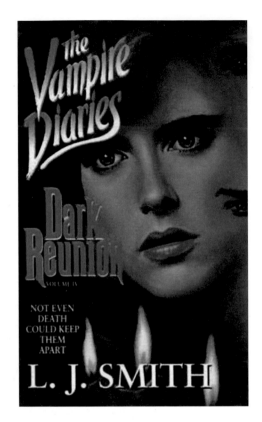

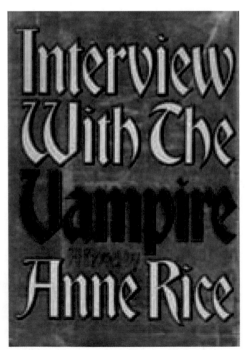

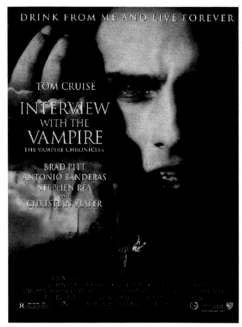

Courtesy of Warner Brothers

writers of vampire tales were beginning to move beyond traditional Gothic settings to explore ways in which the genre would work within areas such as science fiction, the prolific French writer, Gustave Henri Joseph Le Rouge, being a major force in pioneering the genre at this time. In 1908 *Le Prisonnier de la Planète Mars* appeared, and in 1909 Le Rouge produced a sequel, entitled *La Guerre des Vampires*. In *Le Prisonnier de la Planète Mars,* a French engineer, by the name of Robert Darvel, is sent to Mars

the subject. Among the most famous of these is the one concerning the Serbian mill-owner and vampire, Sava Savanovic, whose deeds have been mentioned earlier (*see* page 102 et seq.). He was the inspiration for the story "After Ninety Years," written in the 19th century by the Serbian Milovan Glisic.

In the 20th century, although characters, such as Dracula, were being portrayed in the newly emerging cinema,

by the psychic powers of certain Hindu Brahmins (a caste of Indian scholars and priests). Once on the planet, Darvel encounters and must battle with evil bat-winged bloodsucking creatures that are controlled by an entity known as the Great Brain, which sends Darvel back to Earth, along with some of the bloodsucking creatures. The sequel tells the story of the vampires' war once they arrive on Earth.

Richard Matheson is an American author and screenwriter, working primarily in the fantasy, horror, and

OPPOSITE LEFT: The Vampire Diaries, a young adult series of horror novels written by L.J. Smith.

OPPOSITE CENTER & RIGHT: Anne Rice's novel Interview with the Vampire was made into a movie starring Tom Cruise.

RIGHT: Stephenie Meyer's Twilight Saga became a bestseller after the enormous success of the first Twilight movie.

science fiction genres. He is perhaps best-known as the author of *What Dreams May Come, Somewhere In Time,* and *I Am Legend,* all three of which have been adapted as major motion pictures. *I Am Legend* (1954) is his seminal novel, in which the vampire genre is explored and which also develops the theme of vampirism as a disease. The central character in the book, Robert Neville, is a survivor of a virulent pandemic, the symptoms of which take the form of vampirism. But whereas he seems unaffected, all other survivors appear to have mutated into vampirelike beings.

Neville spends his daylight hours trying to make sense of the apocalypse and searching for countermeasures,

POSTER ART in Twilight

ROBERT PATTINSON & KRISTEN STEWART as seen in The Twilight Saga: New Moon

while at the same time preparing for nightly attacks by vampires by hanging up garlic and boarding up the doors and windows of his house. The interesting paradox is that because he kills those that attack him, they see him as a predator, and fear and loathe him as much as he fears and loathes them. Eventually, captured by his adversaries, Neville swallows some lethal pills. Before he dies, however, the irony is not lost on him that in reality he is the mutant within this new society that has evolved, and that, in time, it is he who will become "legend."

The American author Anne Rice is one of the most successful of the modern proponents of the genre. Her Vampire Chronicles tell of Lestat de Lioncourt, a French nobleman turned vampire, in the 18th century. Most of the books are written in the first person, and we are encouraged to regard the vampire more as an object of pity than an

OPPOSITE: Edward and Bella, the central characters in the Twilight Saga: New Moon.

RIGHT: In New Moon, the character of Jacob (Taylor Lautner) is a werewolf.

POSTER ART in The Twilight Saga: New Moon

MICHAEL SHEEN, CAMERON BRIGHT & JAMIE CAMPBELL BOWER as seen in the Twilight Saga: New Moon

embodiment of evil. Altogether there have been ten volumes, published between 1976 and 2003, the first of which, *Interview with the Vampire*, was adapted as a film starring Tom Cruise, in 1994.

Anne Rice's vampires do not share all the traits that have come to be expected of such creatures. For example, they are neither affected by the usual methods used to repulse them, nor can they be destroyed in the traditional ways. But they

ABOVE: The Volturi is an organized coven of vampires that enforces the laws of the vampire world.

OPPOSITE: Alice uses her ability to see into the future to help Bella when she is in danger.

do possess some reassuringly familiar idiosyncrasies, in that they prefer to sleep in coffins by day, since sunlight causes them pain and even death. They also need blood to sustain them – preferably human blood, although animal blood is acceptable as well. They show little signs of aging, but cannot change their shapes. A few can fly, and they can move at enormous speeds.

Most are able to read the thoughts of mortals and even those of lesser vampires. They possess remarkably keen senses and have great physical strength. These vampires also have other special gifts: they can cause things to catch fire at will; they have an innate, supernatural understanding of any kind of puzzle, machine, or problem; they are artistically talented, having the ability to turn their hands to music, painting, or acting, for example. As alluded to earlier, the reader's empathy with these creatures is enhanced by their emotional and sexual sensitivity as well as by their attractive appearances.

Following on from this new twist on the vampire theme we come to the hugely popular Twilight Saga novels, aimed at the vampire-loving teen and

ASHLEY GREENE as seen in The Twilight Saga: New Moon

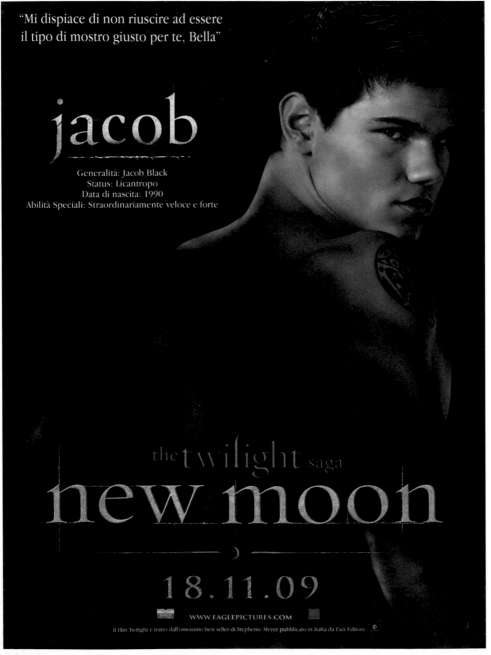

"Mi dispiace di non riuscire ad essere
il tipo di mostro giusto per te, Bella"

jacob

Generalità: Jacob Black
Status: Licantropo
Data di nascita: 1990
Abilità Speciali: Straordinariamente veloce e forte

the twilight saga

new moon

18.11.09

WWW.EAGLEPICTURES.COM

Il film Twilight è tratto dall'omonimo best seller di Stephenie Meyer pubblicato in Italia da Fazi Editore.

POSTER ART in The Twilight Saga: New Moon

young adult market, and with a teenage girl as the central character. The saga consists of four fantasy romance novels, written by the American Stephenie Meyer. They feature the life of Isabella Swan (known as "Bella"), a teenager who falls in love with a 100-year-old vampire called Edward Cullen. The first *Twilight* novel was published in 2005, in which it appears that Bella's love for Edward is fraught with danger, and she is forced to flee from the murderous intentions of another vampire called James. In the second title, *New Moon*, Bella befriends a werewolf called Jacob Black, who tries to defend her against Victoria (the mate of James who was killed by Edward). The third title, *Eclipse,* sees Victoria intent on destroying James's family and then murdering Bella, but James and Jacob join forces and destroy

LEFT: Jacob Black, Bella's werewolf friend, who is also in love with her.

OPPOSITE: Edward, Bella's true love, whom she eventually marries. Edward turns Bella into a vampire in the process of saving her life during childbirth.

Victoria and her vampire army. *Breaking Dawn*, the fourth title, sees Bella and Edward married, but Bella nearly dies giving birth to their daughter. She is only saved when Edward injects Bella with his venom to save her, in the process turning her into a vampire. When the film version of *New Moon* was released in November 2009 it broke box office records, earning £44 million (nearly $71 million) in just 24 hours in the United States, and easily beating the previous record-holder, *Batman: The Dark Night*.

The Irish author Darren Shan (real name Darren O'Shaughnessy) has also produced a series of very successful teen/young adult vampire novels. Called The Saga of Darren Shan, it consists of 12 titles and concerns the boy, Darren Shan, who becomes a half-vampire and the assistant to a full vampire. The first trilogy, entitled *Vampire Blood*, sees Darren coming to terms with his vampirism. The first book in the series, *Cirque du Freak*, was made into a film and released in 2009. In the second trilogy, *Vampire Rites*, Darren attempts to gain the acceptance of the vampire clan and learn about their ways. In the third

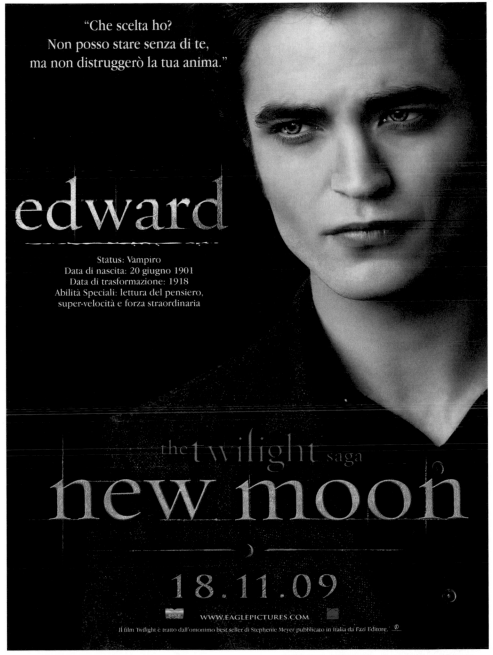

POSTER ART in The Twilight Saga: New Moon

JOHN C. REILLY & CHRIS MASSOGLIA as seen in Cirque du Freak: The Vampire's Assistant

trilogy, *Vampire War,* Darren discovers he may in fact have a greater role to play than he realized in the fate of the vampires and ultimately of the world. The final trilogy, *Vampire Destiny,* sees Darren forced to make some hard decisions and to take his destiny into his own hands.

The vampires in Darren Shan's stories also have a few peculiarities. Instead of biting their prey in order to obtain blood, they use sharp nails to cut veins to release blood, then use their

saliva to staunch the wound. Shan's vampires are rather more benign creatures than the likes of Dracula, and their society has a strict code of conduct, honor, and pride. Interestingly, Shan's vampires are live people rather than reanimated corpses, and they can be killed by several means, although they are incredibly strong and durable, with remarkable powers of healing.

In 2004, John Ajvide Lindqvist's vampire novel, *Let the Right One In,* was published, the story describing the

relationship between a 12-year-old boy, Oskar, and Eli, a centuries-old female vampire child. The book, which was a bestseller in its native Sweden and has also been translated into numerous foreign languages, explores some dark

ABOVE: A still from the 2009 movie, Cirque du Freak: The Vampire's Assistant.

OPPOSITE: Let the Right One In was a Swedish movie released in 2008. An English-language version, Let Me In, premiered in 2010.

aspects of the human condition as well as the world of the supernatural. For example, Eli lives with an older man, Hakan, who takes blood from living victims to give to Eli because he loves her, while issues such as drugs, pedophilia, bullying, theft, murder, and prostitution are also important themes. A Swedish-language film of the book was released in 2008 to widespread acclaim, and another, English-language version, was released in 2010.

The title of the book refers to the aspect of ancient folklore that suggests that a vampire cannot enter a property unless first being invited. Compared with the glut of steamy, sexually implicit teen-focused vampire literature that has been published as well as filmed in recent years, *Let the Right One In* will probably appeal to readers of a more mature age group.

Vampires in Film and Television

Few, if any, other characters have appeared on screen as often as vampires, with portrayals of Dracula being especially pre-eminent. In fact, Dracula has possibly been the subject of more films than any other fictional character.

Even when Dracula is not appearing on screen by name, there is often little doubt that he is the model for the role in question. In the 1960s, for example, an American comedy sitcom, "The Munsters," appeared on television for

the first time. This was a weird and mostly spooky-looking family, headed by a patriarchal Frankenstein's monster lookalike. A running joke in the program is the fact that one member of the family, Marilyn, is in fact beautiful and

LINA LEANDERSSON as seen in Lat den ratte komma in (Let the Right One In)

229

not weird at all, being a Marilyn Monroe lookalike. But because of her non-ghoulish looks, the other family members pity her, considering her to be "not normal." The family grandfather figure, played by Al Lewis, is known as Sam Dracula, Count of Transylvania, and it is clear from his Gothic appearance (dark evening clothes and cape and slicked-back hair) and vampire habits (sleeping in a coffin, sometimes

Courtesy of Universal Studios & CBS

turning into a bat, and so on) that here, indeed, is Dracula in comic guise. The successful television series led to several films, including *Munsters Go Home* (1966) and *The Munsters' Scary Little Christmas* (1996), as well as a host of spin-off merchandise such as model kits and other toys.

OPPOSITE LEFT: Nosferatu (1922).

OPPOSITE RIGHT: The Munster family.

ABOVE: Bela Lugosi in the 1931 version of Dracula.

RIGHT, ABOVE & BELOW: Christopher Lee played the title role in a series of successful Dracula films.

Vampires began to appear in films such as *Vampire of the Coast*, made in 1909, but the most memorable of such depictions, in the days of silent films, was undoubtedly the decidedly creepy 1922 film *Nosferatu*, directed by the influential German film director Friedrich Wilhelm Murnau and starring Max Schreck as the vampire. The plotline was clearly based on the novel *Dracula*, but the film was unlicensed, leading the estate of Bram Stoker to sue the film company for copyright infringement, the outcome being that all copies of the original film were ordered to be destroyed. Since then, experts have

Courtesy of Columbia Pictures

starring the peerless Bela Lugosi as the vampire. It was based on the earlier stage play of the same name, which was itself taken from the Bram Stoker novel. Such was the impact of the film at the time that newspapers reported members of the audiences fainting in shock. *Dracula* proved to be a huge box office hit, paving the way for other horror productions, including sequels to *Dracula* itself, as well as the likes of *Frankenstein, The Mummy,* and *The Wolf Man.*

The original intention had been to cast the American actor Lon Chaney in the role of Dracula in the 1931 production; he had previously appeared in another vampire film in 1927, called *London After Midnight,* but serious illness prevented him from accepting the role. But Lon Chaney's son, Lon Chaney Jr., did star in one of the follow-ups to the original 1931 film; this was *Son of Dracula,* released in 1943.

Other Dracula films followed in the 1940s, including *Abbott and Costello Meet Frankenstein* (1948). Despite its title, Dracula is very much in evidence in this film, played for the second time by Bela Lugosi. As befits a film starring the

American comedy duo, Abbott and Costello, there is also an assortment of other famous horror monsters adding to the general fun and mayhem, including Frankenstein's monster, The Mummy, Wolf Man, and Dr. Jekyll and Mr. Hyde.

In fact, vampires have frequently been portrayed in a less than serious way in films. In addition to Abbott and Costello's offerings, there was the *Fearless Vampire Killers* of 1967, directed by Roman Polanski, while *Old Dracula,* in 1974, featured the famous British actor David Niven as a lovelorn vampire. In 1995 the American actor, Leslie Nielsen, well-known for his many comedy parts, starred in a parody of the Dracula films entitled, *Dracula: Dead and Loving It,* which was directed by Mel Brooks.

Nor were humorous interpretations of Dracula only confined to films, and the British animated television series *Count Duckula* had its first airing in 1988. As the name suggests, it featured a green, vampire duck, attired in a long, purple-lined cloak with a high collar, that lived in spooky Castle Duckula in Transylvania. Based very loosely on the story of Dracula, the story lines often

painstakingly reconstructed the film from a few surviving prints. A notable difference between the vampire Count Orlok in *Nosferatu,* and the classic depiction of Count Dracula, is in the former vampire's appearance. This is no overtly good-mannered, distinguished-looking old nobleman, but a sinister and loathsome creature with pointed ears, protruding teeth, and talon-like fingers.

In 1931 Universal films released *Dracula,* a classic treatment of the legend, directed by Tod Browning and

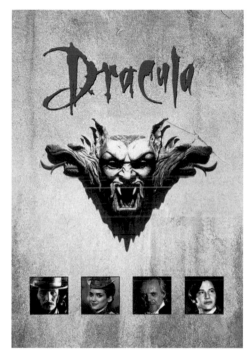

Courtesy of Columbia Pictures

of children's books and an American animated television series.

Returning to films: the 1950s saw another great interpretation, this time by the celebrated Hammer Horror studios. The first of these, *Dracula* (1958), starred the British actor Christopher Lee as the count, which were so successful that seven sequels followed, with Lee appearing in all but two of them, the last of these, in 1973, being *The Satanic Rites of Dracula*. In 1974 there was yet another vampire-related film, *The Legend of the 7 Golden Vampires*, which was ostensibly

centered on Count Duckula's search for riches and fame, assisted by the castle's ability to teleport itself around the world. Another humorous rendering of Dracula is *Little Dracula*, a British series

OPPOSITE: *Leslie Nielson starred in Mel Brooks's Dracula: Dead and Loving It.*

THIS PAGE: *Francis Ford Coppola's Bram Stoker's Dracula came more in the form of a love story. It starred an enigmatic Gary Oldman as the count and Winona Ryder as Mina.*

Courtesy of Columbia Pictures

Courtesy of Columbia Pictures

about Chinese vampires, although Dracula still came into the plot.

Bram Stoker's Dracula (1992), was directed by Francis Ford Coppola and starred Gary Oldman as the vampire. It was indeed based on the novel by Stoker, but has more than a few variations on the original plot, as well as a strong romantic element involving Dracula himself. For example, when Jonathan Harker is at Dracula's castle he shows Dracula a picture of his fiancée, Mina, whom Dracula recognizes as the reincarnation of his long-dead wife! Later in England, appearing as a young

WESLEY SNIPES as seen in Blade II

and handsome man, Dracula succeeds in charming Mina and she admits her love for him. The sexual aspects of vampires have also been highlighted in other films, in which gay and lesbian creatures appear; for example, *Gayracula* (1983) and *Lust for Dracula* (2005).

Since vampires seem so intent on preying on human beings at every available opportunity, it comes as a pleasant surprise to find one dedicated to protecting us from them. Yet this is the premise behind the Blade series of films. Based loosely on the Marvel Comics character, Blade is half-human,

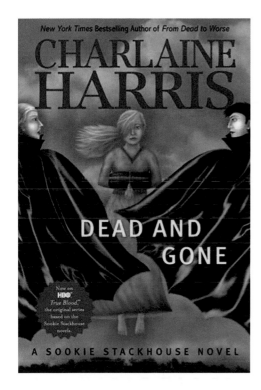

human beings from vampires using a lethal combination of martial arts, firearms, and other weapons, the first film in the series, entitled *Blade*, having been released in 1998. The first of two sequels, *Blade II*, came out in 2002, followed by *Blade: Trinity*, which was released in 2004. Even Dracula himself finds himself featuring in the plotlines of these films as the progenitor of the evil vampires, although here he is known as "Drake."

half-vampire (played by the American actor Wesley Snipes), and protects

OPPOSITE: Wesley Snipes in Blade II.

ABOVE: The successful True Blood TV series is based on Charlaine Harris's Southern Vampire Mysteries.

RIGHT: True Blood features Sookie Stackhouse, a waitress with telepathic skills, who develops a relationship with the vampire Bill Compton.

ANNA PAQUIN & STEPHEN MOYER as seen in True Blood

MICHELLE FORBES & ANNA PAQUIN as seen in True Blood

Developing the vampire theme further, other films have focused on the vampire-hunters themselves, one of the most celebrated of which was *Buffy the Vampire Slayer*, of 1992. Buffy Summers is an American high-school cheerleader who discovers it is her fate to hunt and destroy modern day vampires. The original film starred Kristy Swanson as Buffy, and also featured Donald Sutherland among others.

Buffy is informed by The Watcher (played by Sutherland) that she must be trained to become The Slayer. Eventually she confronts a vampire king, called Lothos (played by Rutger Hauer), which culminates in a clash during the senior dance at Buffy's high school. A television series of the same name was later created and first appeared in 1997, continuing until 2003 and starring Sarah Michelle Gellar as Buffy Summers. The series was somewhat darker than the original film, and produced the spin-off series, *Angel*, in which a vampire has his human soul restored to him by gypsies as a punishment, but subsequently battles with evil forces in an attempt to save souls. The book and magazine industry has produced numerous Buffy-related publications, including novels and comics, and the film, when it was released, took more money at the box office than any other vampire film preceding it.

Yet another American cult vampire series hit the small screen in 2009. The series, *True Blood*, is based on The Southern Vampire Mysteries books by best-selling author Charlaine Harris, which were first published in 2001. Here, Harris creates an alternative history in which the supernatural really exists and where vampires, werewolves, shape-shifters, and other preternatural creatures have suddenly announced their existence, via the medium of television, to the human population. Through the discovery of synthetic blood, the vampires are able to exist without feeding on human beings. Despite this reassuring fact, the vampires' presence is not universally appreciated among the human population. They have many of the traits of the classic vampire, in that they are pale and cold; they can control human minds; they are extremely strong; they are ageless, and some can fly; and they can also be killed by a stake driven through the heart. The vampires have their own kingdoms, each controlled by a vampire king or queen.

True Blood describes the interaction between vampires and humans in a small fictional Louisiana town called Bon Temps. The main female character, Sookie Stackhouse (played by Anna Paquin), is a waitress with telepathic powers who develops a relationship with Bill Compton, one of the vampires (played by Stephen Moyer). Handsome and youthful though he may appear, being a vampire, he just happens to be 173 years old. Set in America's Deep South, *True Blood* combines our fear of vampires and the dark forces with our abiding interest in the lives and loves of others, resulting in a kind of steamy soap opera with fangs. It seems to be a winning formula, for the first season of the series won a Golden Globe award as well as an Emmy (the television equivalent of an Oscar).

OPPOSITE: Maryann Forrester and Sookie Stackhouse, characters in the TV series True Blood.

ENVOI

We have now reached the end of our journey into the realm of the vampire, and it must be for the reader to decide wherein lies the truth. Do these creatures of the night truly exist, and should we be in mortal fear of being subjected to such dreadful visitations at any time? Or are vampires nothing more

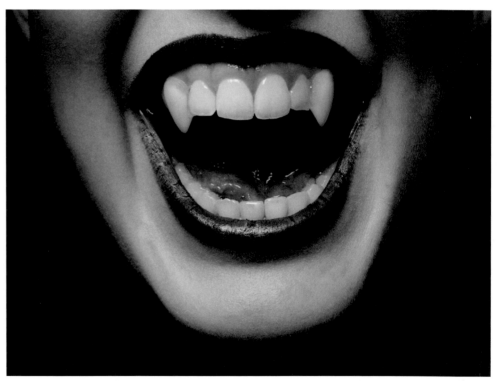

than the wild imaginings of peasant folk, to be dismissed simply as the myths and legends of superstitious people?

It is true that solid evidence for the existence of vampires has so far proved elusive; yet surely this is to be expected?

Why would such an entity show itself to all and sundry, and thus risk its own destruction? Surely it is better instead to

Real or myth, vampires never fail to fascinate, terrify, and enthrall us.

238

move in the shadows, use all manner of subterfuge, and attack the unwary as they sleep? And if such a creature is the stuff of pure fantasy, why has the notion of the vampire asserted itself so frequently and in so many different cultures?

On the other hand, if vampires are so rampant in the world, where are all the victims of their evil deeds or even the disciples of the cult? Or perhaps there are more vampires living among us than we truly know? For all this, our safe, modern world seems an eternity away from the old vampire haunts of places such as the mist-shrouded mountains of Transylvania, and most of us might consider ourselves immune from these deadly wanderers of the night. But perhaps it would be wise to draw that blanket more closely up around our necks before we surrender to sleep – just in case!

Modern-day vampires are a world apart from those of remote Transylvanian villages. What were once bloodsucking monsters are today drinking synthetic or animal blood and stealing the hearts of teenage girls. Could it be, however, that such entities actually exist?

GLOSSARY

Apotropaic An adjective used to describe any object, chant, ceremony, or similar ritual that is designed to ward off evil spirits or bad luck.

Apotropaism The use of magic spells, signs, amulets, rituals, and so on designed to ward off evil spirits or bad luck.

Attila the Hun The emperor of the Huns (a group of Eurasian nomads) from 434 to 453. At its height, his empire stretched from Germany to the Ural River, and from the Danube River to the Baltic Sea. He was one of the most feared of all military leaders, infamous in his ruthlessness, cunning, and single-mindedness in his pursuit of military conquests. Count Dracula proudly claims to be his direct descendant.

Bran Castle A Gothic and Renaissance fortress in southern Transylvania, near to Brasov, originally erected in the 13th century. It is now a tourist attraction and part of Romania's Dracula tourist trail, although there is no real evidence linking the castle to a personnage by the name of Dracula.

Cannibal Any animal, and this may include a human being, that eats the body parts of one of its own kind.

Cannibalism The act of eating the body parts of one's own species.

Carpathian Mountains The largest mountain range in Europe, forming an arc about 932 miles (1500 km) long across central and eastern Europe. In the Southern Carpathians of Romania, the peaks reach a height of more than 8,202 ft. (2500 m). The Carpathians have long been the habitat of brown bears, wolves, and other species..

Catacomb An underground cemetery or burial place, often with tunnels, and with rooms or recesses for individual coffins.

Corpse A dead body.

Crucifix A Latin cross, upon which the figure of Jesus is seen crucified. This important Christian symbol is reputed to be a powerful tool in the fight against vampires.

Decapitation The act of cutting off the head from the body. A favorite method of destroying suspected vampires among some peasant communities.

Decomposition The biological process that occurs after the death of an organism, resulting in the ultimate breakdown of body tissues through the action of bacteria and other agents.

GLOSSARY

Demon In folklore, religion, and superstition, a supernatural being in the form of a malevolent spirit.

Disinterment The act of taking something from out of the ground, especially a buried corpse.

Dracula, Count A mythical vampire, made famous in the novel of the same name by the Irish author Bram Stoker.

Entity Something that has real existence.

Garlic A pungent, strong-tasting bulb, used in cooking and medicine, that is also used as a defense against vampires.

Ghost The spirit of a deceased person said to appear in visible form. Ghosts are reputed to haunt the particular locations with which they had associations when the person was alive.

Gothic Describes a style of imposing, sometimes gloomy, architecture that flourished from the late Medieval Period. It is the style used in many churches, cathedrals, palaces, and castles, for example, and features tall walls, pointed arches, flying buttresses, and rib vaulting. Many Gothic buildings also feature grotesques and gargoyles – evil-looking, mythical creatures that are supposed to have a protective function.

Headhunter A member of any tribe of people that indulges in the procurement of human heads for religious purposes or as war trophies. Within some tribes, the cult of headhunting may sometimes be linked with cannibalism.

Holy water Water that has been blessed by a priest, and which is sometimes used to ward off or combat vampirism.

Incubus A male demon believed to have sexual intercourse with sleeping women. In many religions it is said that repeated intercourse with an incubus can result in sickness or even death.

Mausoleum An impressive building housing a tomb or group of tombs

Pagan A person holding religious beliefs other than those of the main world religions. Also used as an adjective.

Poenari Castle A ruined castle in Romania in the Arges river valley, now partly rebuilt as a tourist attraction. Once used by Vlad III Tepes (Vlad the Impaler) as his stronghold, and the scene of some of his impalings.

Poltergeist A ghost or other supernatural being, supposedly responsible for physical disturbances, such as making loud noises and throwing objects about.

Porphyria A disease that produces symptoms similar to those seen in cases of suspected vampirism.

Preternatural That which appears outside or beyond the normal.

Renaissance The revival of European art, architecture, and literature under the influence of Classical Greek and Roman models in the 14th–16th centuries.

Revenant One who returns after death in the form of a spirit such as a ghost or a vampire.

VAMPIRE LEGENDS AND MYTHS

Rosary A string of prayer beads used for keeping count of the prayers making up this form of religious devotion; a popular element of Roman Catholicism and of some other religions.

Shape-shifter In the context of mythology, superstition, and science fiction, a person or being with the ability to change their physical form at will. Vampires, for example, are said to transform themselves, on occasions, into bats or wolves.

Spirit A supernatural, incorporeal entity. Also, the vital element of a living creature that animates its body, i.e., the soul.

Succubus A female demon believed to have sexual intercourse with sleeping men.

Tomb An excavation in rock or soil, a grave or a mausoleum, used for the interment of a dead body.

Transylvania A large tableland region of north-western Romania, separated from the rest of the country by the Carpathian Mountains. It is a place steeped in legend and the focus for many myths and tales of vampires, including the famous novel *Dracula*.

Undead A collective term used to describe any of the beings of mythology, myth, or legend that have died but which continue to behave as if they were still alive, and include vampires, zombies, and ghosts.

Vampire In myth and legend, a corpse that cannot rest in its grave, but reanimates itself by rising up to feed on the lifeblood of living creatures, especially human beings.

Vampirism The act of behaving like a vampire.

Vlad Tepes or Vlad the Impaler A ruler of Wallachia, a former principality of south-eastern Europe, between the Danube and the Transylvanian Alps, which united with Moldavia in 1861 to form Romania. Also known as Vlad III or Vlad Dracula, he reigned briefly from about 1448, and again from 1456 to 1462. His reign was characterized by acts of extreme cruelty towards both his enemies and his own people. He infamously impaled his victims alive on stakes, for which he gained the name, Vlad the Impaler. He was also the inspiration for the name of the vampire in Bram Stoker's novel *Dracula*.

Voodoo A form of religion originating in Africa but also practiced in parts of the Caribbean (such as Haiti) and elsewhere.

Werewolf A person said to be able to shape-shift into a wolf or wolflike creature, usually when there is a full moon.

Zombie A corpse said to be revived by witchcraft, especially in some African and Caribbean religions.

FOR MORE INFORMATION

The Bram Stoker Memorial Association
Penthouse North
Suite 145
29 Washington Square West
New York, NY 10011-9180
Web site:
http://www.benecke.com/stoker.html
This is an association for Dracula and
Bram Stoker enthusiasts.

The Dracula Society
PO Box 30848
London W12 0GY
England
http://www.thedraculasociety.org.uk/about
thesociety.html
Formed in 1973, this society hosts
meetings, events, and travel opportunities,
such as trips to Transylvania, for people
interested in vampire lore.

Museum of the Moving Image
36-01 35 Avenue
Astoria, New York 11106
(718) 777-6888
Web site: http://www.movingimage.us
The museum contains a large collection of
horror movie memorabilia, in addition to
artifacts from various other film genres.
The collections are devoted to the art,
history, technique, and technology of the
moving image.

The Official Twilight Fan Club
http://www.facebook.com/group.php?gid
=21257565758
This is fan club on Facebook dedicated to
the popular Twilight series.

Romanian Culture Institute New York
200 East Thirty-eighth Street
New York, NY 10016
(212) 687-0180
Web site: http://www.icrny.org/index.html
The Romanian Culture Institute has an
extensive library and numerous resources
for researching Romanian arts and culture.

Romanian Folk Art Museum
1606 Spruce Street
Philadelphia, PA 19103
(215) 732-6780
Web site: http://www.romanianculture.us
Established in 1983, the Romanian Folk
Art Museum exhibits a vast collection of
folkloric artifacts.

The Rosenbach Museum and Library
2008-2010 Delancey Place
Philadelphia, PA 19103
(215) 732-1600
Web site: http://www.rosenbach.org
Each October, the Rosenbach, which
houses Bram Stoker's original research,
notes, and outlines for Dracula, presents a
month-long celebration, The Dracula
Festival, inspired by Stoker's work.

Spellbound Museum
192 Essex Street
Salem, MA 01970
(978) 745-0138
Web site:
http://www.spellboundtours.com/spellbou
nd_museum.htm
The Spellbound Museum offers tours that
include local vampire lore and maintains a
small museum with vampire-related artifacts.

Transylvanian Society of Dracula (TSD)
Canadian Chapter, TSD
2309-397 Front Street W
Toronto, ON M5V 3S1
Canada
Web site: http://blooferland.com/tsd.html
This society is a nonprofit organization
dedicated to the study of both the fictional
Count Dracula and Vlad the Impaler.
There are also chapters of the TSD
throughout Romania and other countries
in Europe.

The Vampire Diaries Canada
Web site:
http://thevampirediariescanada.com
This fansite from Canada brings
enthusiasts of the Vampire Diaries series
(based on books by L. J. Smith) together to
share their love of the TV show.

Vampire Diaries Fan Club Blog
http://vampirediariesfanclubblog.
blogspot.com
This blog is dedicated to the Vampire
Diaries television show.

Web Sites

Due to the changing nature of Internet
links, Rosen Publishing has developed an
online list of Web sites related to the subject
of this book. This site is updated regularly.
Please use this link to access the list:

http://www.rosenlinks.com/snat/vamps

FOR FURTHER READING

Bartlett, Wayne, and Flavia Idriceanu. *Legends of Blood: The Vampire in History and Myth.* Santa Barbara, CA: Greenwood Publishing Group, 2006.

Bennett, Adelaide. *Global Legends & Lore: Vampires & Werewolves Around the World* (Making of a Monster: Vampires & Werewolves). Broomall, PA: Mason Crest Publishers, 2010.

Beresford, Matthew. *From Demons to Dracula: The Creation of the Modern Vampire Myth.* London, UK: Reaktion Books, 2009.

Clements, Susannah. *The Vampire Defanged: How the Embodiment of Evil Became a Romantic Hero.* Grand Rapids, MI: Brazos Press, 2011.

Cybulski, Angela. *Vampires: Fact or Fiction?* Farmington Hills, MI: Greenhaven Press, 2003.

Gee, Joshua. *Encyclopedia Horrifica: The Terrifying TRUTH! About Vampires, Ghosts, Monsters and More.* New York, NY: Scholastic, 2007.

Goldberg, Enid A., and Norman Itzkowitz. *Vlad the Impaler: The Real Count Dracula.* London, UK: Franklin Watts, 2009.

Grahame-Smith, Seth. *Abraham Lincoln: Vampire Hunter.* New York, NY: Grand Central Publishing, 2010.

Guiley, Rosemary Ellen. *Vampires* (Mysteries, Legends, and Unexplained Phenomena). New York, NY: Checkmark Books, 2009.

Hamby, Zachary. *Mythology for Teens: Classic Myths for Today's World.* Austin, TX: Prufrock Press, 2009.

Hamilton, John. *Vampires.* Edina, MN: Abdo Publishing, 2007.

Hofer, Charles. *Meet Dracula* (Famous Movie Monsters). New York, NY: Rosen Publishing Group, Inc., 2005.

Humphries, C.C. *Vlad: The Last Confession.* London, UK: Orion Publishing Group, Ltd, 2009.

Jacobson, Sid, and Ernie Colon. *Vlad the Impaler: The Man Who Was Dracula.* New York, NY: Hudson Street Press, 2009.

Jinks, Catherine. *The Reformed Vampire Support Group.* New York, NY: Harcourt Children's Books, 2009.

Kallen, Stuart A. *Vampire History and Lore* (Vampire Library). Reprint ed. San Diego, CA: ReferencePoint Press, 2010.

Kallen, Stuart A. *Vampires* (Mysterious & Unknown). San Diego, CA: ReferencePoint Press, 2008.

Karg, Barb, Arjean Spaite, and Rick Sutherland. *The Everything Vampire Book: From Vlad the Impaler to the Vampire Lestat—a History of Vampires in Literature, Film, and Legend.* Avon, MA: Adams Media, 2009.

Kostova, Elizabeth. *The Historian.* Boston, MA: Little, Brown and Company, 2005.

Krensky, Stephen. *Vampires.* Minneapolis, MN: Lerner Publications Company, 2007.

Martin, Dawn. *Vampires.* Duncan, SC: Hammond Undercover, 2009.

McMeans, Bonnie. *Vampires.* Farmington Hills, MI: Kidhaven Press, 2006.

Meyer, Stephenie. *Twilight.* New York, NY: Little, Brown Books for Young Readers, 2005.

Miller, Elizabeth. *A Dracula Handbook.* Bloomington, IN: Xlibris Corporation, 2005.

Miller, Elizabeth. *Dracula: Sense & Nonsense.* Essex, UK: Desert Island Books, 2000.

Miller, Raymond. *Vampires.* Farmington Hills, MI: KidHaven Press, 2005.

Rook, Sebastian. *The Vampire Plagues.* London, 1850. New York, NY: Scholastic, 2005.

Sloan, Christopher. *Bury the Dead: Tombs, Corpses, Mummies, Skeletons, and Rituals.* Washington, DC: National Geographic Society, 2002.

Smith, L. J., *The Vampire Diaries: The Awakening.* Rev. pbk. ed. New York, NY: HarperTeen, 2009.

Stefoff, Rebecca. *Vampires, Zombies, and Shape-Shifters* (Secrets of the Supernatural). Tarrytown, NY: Marshall Cavendish Benchmark, 2008.

Stoker, Dacre, and Ian Holt. *Dracula The Un-Dead.* Reprint ed. New York, NY: NAL Trade, 2010.

Summers, Montague. *Vampires and Vampirism.* Mineola, NY: Dover Publications, 2005.

Trow, M.J. *Vlad the Impaler: In Search of the Real Dracula.* Gloucestershire, UK: The History Press, 2004.

The Vampire Book. New York, NY: DK Publishing, 2009.

Wallace, Anne Sharp. *The Gypsies.* Farmington Hills, MI: Lucent Books, 2002.

Wright, Dudley. *The Book of Vampires* (Dover Books on Anthropology and Folklore). 2nd ed. New York, NY: Dover Publications, 2006.

Wright, Dudley. *Vampires and Vampirism: Legends From Around the World.* Maple Shade, NJ: Lethe Press, 2001.

INDEX

INDEX

INDEX

ABOUT THE AUTHOR

Derek Hall is a graduate of London University. He has written more than twenty-five popular books for both adults and children, and has added his contributions, both in print and as part of radio broadcasts, to various topics.

VAMPIRE LEGENDS AND MYTHS

ACKNOWLEDGMENTS

155 Alex Panoiu, page 91: Olga Pavlosky, page 123: Pdinnen, page 124: Luis Perez, page 138: Pizzodisevo, page 97, 122, 141 left: Radio Nederland Werelomroep: page 10 top left: Matt Rheinbold, page 71, 195: Tambako the Jaguar, page 180: Technotr: page 15 top: Tiago Ribeiro, page 119: Rightindex, page 129: Andres Rodriguez: page 114, 115, 116, 114: Rusticus80, page 174: Shadoegate, page 15 below right: Spisharam - away, page 18 Sean Toyer, page 86: Harikrishnan Tulsidas, Page 142: Brian Scott, page 49: Sochotnicky, page 50: Jan Sokoly, page 75: Kit Smith, page 74 right: Supa_pedro, page 80: Swaminatuan, page 135: Tatu_aka.T: page 90: TheeErin, page 203: Carsten Tolkmit, page 64: Christopher Walker, page 110: James Whitesmith, page 85, 179: Jack Wolf, page 172: David Wright.

The following images are supplied by Wikipedia Common. and the following photographers: Page 9 left: Acatenazzi. page 134: Shawn Allen: page 11 above: Alvesgaspar, page 156: Jan Ainali, page 34: Radovan Bahna, Page 162: Elena Chochkova, page 84: Dimitir, page 132: Jayan466: page 38: Jialiang Gao, page 175: Adam Jones, page 53: Laslovarga, page 20 above Moros, page 41, 106: National Portrait Gallery, page 20 below: Oxyman, page 10 below left, 13 both, page 22 both, page 23 above, page 28, page 35 both, 40 both, 55 both right, 56, 59 right, 60, 81 both, 120, 127, 128, 130 both, 133, 144, 145 both, 153, 158 both, 178 right, 185, 186, 190 right, 191 left, 201, 215, 219 left: Public Domain, page 82: Rémih, page 11 below: Stan Shebs, page 10 right: Shizhao, page 190 left: Valimane, page 74 left: Leo de Vos, page 51, 54: Ivan Yakovleich/ Ivan Bilbin, page 25: Manfred Werner Tsui, page 178 left: Ian Woodward, page 15 below left: H Zell, Page 12: Fortean Picture Library.

Page 28, 230 all: Universal Pictures
Page 221 right: Warner Brothers
Page 229 right: Universal Pictures & CBS.
Page 231, 232 all: Columbia Pictures

The following images are supplied by Capital Pictures: page 23: below: Capital pictures/CAST of Buffy The Vampire Slayer, page 218: Capital Pictures/CAST of Buffy The Vampire Slayer, page 219: right: Capital Pictures/POSTER ART in I Am Legend, page 221: right: Capital Pictures/POSTER ART in Twilight, pages 222: Capital pictures/ROBERT PATTINSON & KRISTEN STEWART as seen in The Twilight Saga: New Moon, page 234: Capital pictures/MICHAEL SHEEN, CAMERON BRIGHT & JAMIE CAMPBELL BOWER as seen in The Twilight Saga: New Moon, page 234: Capital pictures/ASHLEY GREENE as seen in The Twilight Saga: New Moon, page 223, 266, 227: Capital pictures/POSTER ART in The Twilight Saga: New Moon, page 228: Capital Pictures/JOHN C. REILLY & CHRIS MASSOGLIA as seen in Cirque du Freak: The Vampire's Assistant, page 229: Capital Pictures/LINA LEANDERSSON as seen in Lat den ratte komma in (Let the Right One In), page 234: WESLEY SNIPES as seen in Blade II, page 236: Capital Pictures/ANNA PAQUIN & STEPHEN MOYER as seen in True Blood, page 236: Capital Pictures/MICHELLE FORBES & ANNA PAQUIN as seen in True Blood.

Additional credits: p. 33 Private Collection/Cooley Gallery, Old Lyme, Connecticut, USA/The Bridgeman Art Library; p. 43 Shutterstock.com; p. 55 © Kathy Gold/Purestock/SuperStock; p. 57 © Christie's Images Ltd./SuperStock.